SIMPLY BARBARA BUSH

SIMPLY BARBARA BUSH

A PORTRAIT OF AMERICA'S CANDID FIRST LADY

DONNIE RADCLIFFE

WARNER BOOKS

A Warner Communications Company

Warner Books, Inc., 666 Fifth Avenue, New York, NY 10103
W A Warner Communications Company

Printed in the United States of America
Book design by H. Roberts

Quality Printing and Binding by:
Berryville Graphics
P.O. Box 272
Berryville, VA 22611 U.S.A.

For my family, those who are here—
Bob, Don, Bobbe, Jennifer,
Donnel, Hadley, Ruth, and Irene—
and those who are not.

Acknowledgments

*S*ome are colleagues, some are friends, some are
people I have never met, but all gave assistance
in one way or another so that this book could
be written. I am indebted to them for sharing their
recollections, experiences, guidance, and time.

I am deeply grateful to the *Washington Post* and
to Mary Hadar, the editor of Style where I am a
reporter, for the tolerance shown me in this endeavor.
Many of my colleagues there were especially helpful
and encouraging, in particular Robin Groom, Peat
O'Neil, David Hoffman, Ann Devroy, Lou Cannon,
Ellen Edwards, Kathy Wall, and Melissa Mathis.

Scores of people from many periods of Barbara Bush's life shared information generously, but in particular I want to thank Vic Gold, Craig Fuller, Sheila Tate, Mary Anne Fackelman-Miner, Landon Parvin, Jack Steele, Pete Roussel, James E. Duffy, Margot Woodwell, Jinx Crouch, Ruth Graves, Thomas W.L. Ashley, Betsy Heminway, Janet Steiger, Mary Ann Stewart, Shirley Pettis Roberson, Cordelia Lambert Stites, Shavaun Robinson Towers, Rosanne Morgan Clarke, June Biedler, and Susan Estey Edgerly.

Susan Porter Rose, Anna Perez, Sondra Haley, Jean Becker, and Jay Suchan on Barbara Bush's staff at the White House were invaluable, lending enormous assistance throughout. They all merit special thanks. I am also grateful to others at the White House, including Janet McConnell, David Valdez, Don Rhodes, and Alixe Glen.

Members of Mrs. Bush's family were extremely cooperative and forthcoming, and I am especially indebted to her brother Scott Pierce, who went out of his way on numerous occasions to lend assistance.

Others who added much to this endeavor were Marguerite Sullivan, Carl Sferrazza Anthony, Joyce Czajkowski, Earl Miller, and Anne Douglas Milburn. The project itself would never have happened without Megan Rosenfeld, Gail E. Ross, and James D. Frost.

In addition, there were three very special people, all contributing something unique. Barbara Feinman, a veteran of this book-writing business, provided expertise without which I would have been hopelessly lost. Sandy Flickner, a gifted editor at the *Washington*

Post, gave unparalleled encouragement and professional assistance. Finally, Barbara Bush, a woman of enormous energy, somehow managed to find a place for me in her schedule during those first busy days of her husband's administration. She knew the general scope of this book but until it was published had no way of knowing how it turned out.

Contents

Preface

hen it was suggested that I write a book about Barbara Bush, my first reaction was that it was premature to take a serious look at a woman whose husband had been president less than a month, and in particular, to draw any conclusions about her performance as First Lady. I recognized that she seemed to have captured the public imagination, but I was inclined to write some of that off as postinaugural euphoria.

There is a tendency in partisan Washington to reach a conclusion before there is evidence to support it. I didn't doubt that Barbara was a compassionate, caring, outspoken, and candid woman, but I did have problems adding them up and getting the answer some people were getting at that point, that she was the conscience of the Bush White House.

The more I thought about Barbara Bush, however, the more curious I was about her childhood, her parents, her family life, and the forces and events that combined to make her the woman she became. In one of several interviews I had with her during the 1988 presidential campaign, I noted that I really had read very little about her early life. She seemed quite surprised that it should matter. "What have I ever done that would make you read about me?" she asked. In contemplating this project, I remembered that remark and decided that I wanted to find out. She hadn't always been the grandmotherly white-haired and wrinkled woman Americans had come to identify with stability and traditional family values.

As I saw it, writing a book about her didn't pose any more problems for me as an author than as a reporter who covered her for the *Washington Post*. What did concern me was whether in the time allotted me I would ever learn the answers I needed. Certainly there was no immediate response from the White House when I made my initial inquiry about whether Barbara would cooperate. I could only suppose that part of the delay was the crush of events demanding attention in those early days of getting settled. But I also suspected that Barbara hadn't yet come to grips with her new visibility and the enormous interest people had in her. I knew the idea that she might figure prominently in books being written was not one that would necessarily appeal to her.

She is stubborn but she is also realistic, and recognizing, perhaps, that there was more to be gained by adding her own voice than by leaving the voices of others to speculate about answers to some questions, she agreed to talk to me. The times we were together were never long enough—I often left the White House with as many new questions as the ones I had arrived with—but I always came away feeling she had earnestly tried to shed some light on this other Barbara few of us knew.

Once I asked her if her mother had had a sense of humor. She answered unhesitatingly that she hadn't, but later she was obviously bothered by her quick response because at lunch that same day she asked an old friend of her mother's about it. The friend assured her that Pauline Pierce had had no sense of humor.

I learned that some of the things she said didn't always come out of her mouth the way she later wished they had. When she and President Bush went to Europe in late May 1989, she told a group of reporters that there would be "no page-turner" among books about her. A few weeks later in a receiving line at the White House, I hadn't yet been released from George Bush's handshake when she was saying to me, "Oh, I was so worried your feelings would be hurt by what I said about your book!" I assured her that I knew precisely what she had meant, and I had—that her self-effacing way had once again gotten the better of her.

The challenge in writing about Barbara Bush was in portraying her as human, as neither sainted humanitarian nor model wife and mother. "If you're looking for dirt, you'll only find lint," Christopher Buckley, author and a former George Bush speechwriter, warned shortly after I started the book.

"What you see is what you get," was how her family described her, which in the end may have been the most balanced interpretation of all, because what you saw and got was a sympathetic and gentle woman who could also be feisty and sarcastic. "I'm neither better nor worse than anybody else," Barbara told me in May 1989, the last time we talked for this book, and after twenty years of watching First Ladies move in and out of the White House, I could hardly argue about that.

My first interview with her in 1980 came shortly after Ronald Reagan chose George Bush as his running mate. She and I sat in the garden of the house the Bushes were renting in northwest Washington, and while I don't recall that she was as witty and relaxed as I later found her to be, I do remember that she was direct.

"I'm assuming everybody knows that I thought George would be the best-qualified person for president. I haven't changed on that," she said. "But I'm thrilled that if it couldn't be George, it's Governor Reagan. And I'm surprised about that, but I'm very truthful about that."

I also got my first glimpse of how cutting a candidate's wife she could be. "I think Mrs. Carter has to be the bravest woman in the world to take herself to Detroit and campaign for her husband," she said of Rosalynn Carter. "I believe in being supportive to your husband—and she must love him a bunch—but I'd have been scared to death if that had been George Bush and I had to go to a city where they had forty percent unemployment with minorities and stand up and tell them my husband had been good and things were getting better. There's nothing wrong with being a strong, supportive wife—if you have a strong husband. I think she missed on that. I think I'm strong. It's not a quality I would have aimed for, but I think I am."

Eight years later, the target was Michael Dukakis and also his strength. And she finished him off with: "There's no question that Mike Dukakis is a fabulous debater. You got to have card sense, too, in life. I know a lot of people who got all A's in school but couldn't cope with life. I'm not saying that Mike Dukakis is that, because he certainly is one of two people seeking the highest job in the land and I think he's very bright. And being one of two is something."

Going to see Barbara at the White House was an experience absent of formality. One day I arrived as she was coming off the elevator. "Want to see the puppies?" she asked. And guiding me through the Diplomatic Entrance to the South Lawn, we walked toward a playpen where Millie's offspring were basking—and doing other things—in the spring sunshine. "Hmm," Barbara murmured after taking a close look at the lawn, "maybe it's time to move them to another spot."

Inside the White House, she welcomed me into the family quarters. I hadn't been invited there since Rosalynn Carter was First Lady. After covering Nancy Reagan for eight years, and interviewing her in the White House Library, the Map Room, or some other near and distant place, I finally "graduated" for our last get-together in January 1989 to the elegant and formal Yellow Oval Room upstairs—where I'd had my first interview with Pat Nixon twenty years earlier. I thought the choice of settings for all of those interviews said a lot about those five First Ladies.

The White House had been painful at times for Nancy Reagan, and by her own later admission she had had to learn how to live there. Such, however, was not Barbara Bush's problem. After twenty-three years in and out of Washington, she knew that 1600 Pennsylvania Avenue was her kind of place.

Donnie Radcliffe
McLean, Virginia
June 1989

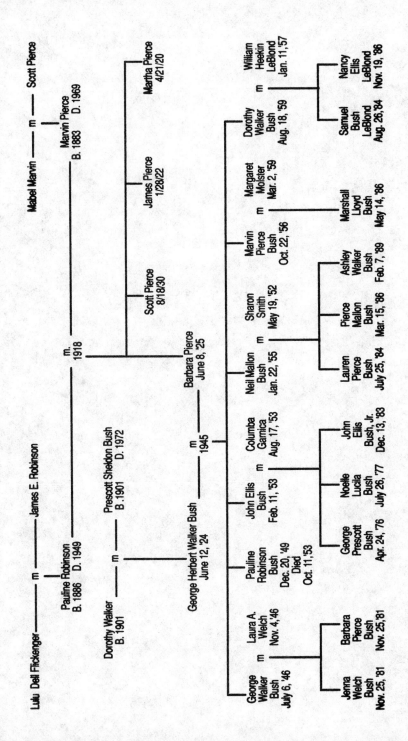

1

Wrinkles and All

"My mail tells me a lot of fat, white-haired, wrinkled ladies are tickled pink."

*G*eorge Bush was in the final stretch of the 1988 presidential campaign, with reason to feel good. Though there were ten days to go to the election, he was ahead in the polls. He wasn't saying much, just sitting there in his cabin aboard Air Force Two listening to campaign aides predicting that he would win. Suddenly, his voice silenced the others. "I don't know about that," he said. "But if I do [win], there's one prediction I'll make, and that's that America will fall in love with Barbara Bush."

America did.

In no time at all, her white hair, her wrinkles, her size-14 figure, and her fake pearls became the new standards by which American women could measure themselves—and hope to measure up. After eight years of Nancy Reagan and Clairol's Moon Gold, size-4 Adolfos, and real Harry Winston jewels, Americans had a down-to-earth First Lady who, it seemed, wouldn't have changed even if she could have. Long before the campaign had begun, she acknowledged those differences, working them to her advantage. In a 1986 speech at Saints and Sinners, an annual insiders' roast for Washington charities, she met Nancy's glamorous image head-on: "As you know, we have a lot in common," she said. "She adores her husband; I adore mine. She fights drugs; I fight illiteracy. She wears a size three . . . so's my leg."

Her recognition factor at the start of the campaign had been so low she vowed if she ever wrote a book she would call it *Will the Woman in the Red Dress Please Get Out of the Picture?* because that's what a photographer had yelled during a San Antonio rally when she was standing next to Bush. "I looked down at my dress and I thought, 'My Lord, it's me.' "

She wasn't unknown for long. Nobody worked harder to get George Bush elected, and she allowed herself to be thrust into the public eye. But there were limits, and Barbara made her position clear to Roger Ailes, Bush's campaign media adviser. "I'll do anything you want, but I won't dye my hair, change my wardrobe, or lose weight."

There was no need of that. If Ailes had had to invent her, he could not have done a better job. "People want straight talk. In a sense, a woman and her time have come together. Barbara Bush didn't try to fit in in the 1960s and '70s. She's who she's always been," Ailes told the *New York Times* after the election. "She feels people should age gracefully and not get frantic."

Barbara Bush seemed too good to be true. Here was a woman who could not only do her own hair and iron her own clothes but also fix a leaky water pipe, rewire an outlet, and make minor car repairs. She played cagey tennis, baby-sat the grandchildren, gave the middle of the bed to the dog, and worried more about her garden than whether she got dirt under her fingernails. She also avoided high society and when she thought she could get away with it, threw protocol to the winds.

That wasn't all: Here was a First Lady who professed to care more about where people slept at night and what they ate, whether their children learned to read and if anybody was looking after them, than whether she gained thirteen pounds, wore the same old clothes, or looked a fright in pictures. ("The worst one of me came out in Detroit. You could have planted a whole potato field in the rows of wrinkles," she said.)

Barbara kept up a running banter with photographers. "If you show wrinkles, you're through for life," she'd warn. And she made fun of herself: "Unfortunately, my winning smile makes me look as if I'm being electrocuted. My kids are always looking at photographs of me and saying, 'Look at Mom, she's plugged in again!' "

On the campaign trail, where her competition, Kitty Dukakis, symbolized the woman of the nineties, Barbara fearlessly played up her "grandmother" image; after all, she had ten grandchildren of her own, and another on the way. "I'm everybody's grandmother," she would say to all, including recovering alcoholics and drug addicts with whom she sometimes sat and prayed. "It's the gray-haired ladies who come up and say 'Gee, you look exactly like my mother' that worry me a bit. But I don't mind. The truth is, if I've learned nothing in my thousand years, I've learned that you really shouldn't judge a book by its cover."

As early as 1980, the first time George Bush ran for president, people had suggested she dye her hair a "younger" shade. The idea annoyed her. "It makes me mad as the dickens," she told Barbara Gamarekian of the *New York Times* shortly after George was sworn in as vice president. "If I did something like that, I think all of America would fall flat on its face from astonishment."

Barbara had started to go gray in her late twenties when Robin, her second-born, was dying of leukemia. Though George never asked her to dye her hair, his mother did ask her, when Barbara was in her midthirties. So she dyed it, and as Gail Sheehy learned in a 1988 interview for *Vanity Fair*, she continued to dye it even when the brown shade turned green every time she swam in a pool. She decided to call a halt the summer of 1970. Why *then*, asked Sheehy, particularly when other women in their midforties were working harder than ever to look younger? "George Bush never noticed. So why had I gone through those years of agony?" Barbara explained to me later, "I meant it as George likes me for what I am, and not what color my hair is."

She thought that people who worried about their hair all the time were "boring." "I wash my hair every day of my life and probably washed all the color out. But I can exercise, play tennis. I don't ever have to say to George, 'I'm sorry, I can't do that, I just got my hair done.' You have to have priorities in life and that's just not one I have. What you see is what you get." Her only recorded bow to vanity was substituting contact lenses for glasses "because I looked older than my husband." She claimed that the only thing that kept her from being just another face in the crowd was her Secret Service detail causing a flurry while trying to protect her.

There were those "rows of wrinkles," carved not just by forty-five summers spent on a windswept Maine coast or beneath a withering Texas sun, but by the emotions of a woman who never was very skillful at concealing her feelings, whether amusement, disgust, or sorrow. There was nothing to be done about the wrinkles, but here again, people volunteered their opinions. One woman suggested that the reason they showed up so prominently on television during the Republican convention in New Orleans in August 1988 was that she had slept on the pillow wrong, creasing her face. "What I would like to tell her is that the wrinkles came not from sleeping but from not getting any sleep at all," Barbara wrote in her "Campaign Diary" that ran weekly in *USA Today* as the election approached.

And there were those matronly clothes. She ventured that one thing she would never need to worry about—though, of course, she would be proven wrong—was "standing there [at a White House function] and having people say, 'Who did her gown?' " She sidestepped passing judgment on the potentially explosive issue of Nancy Reagan's borrowed designer clothes with a matter-of-fact answer that she bought all her clothes—with one exception, and George had reported that gift dress on his financial disclosure form.

Nobody accused her of being chic, much less a candidate for the annual best-dressed list. "It takes a lot of strain off you," she once said of her unfashionable image. Still, Barbara was certain to have an effect on Seventh Avenue, the center of America's garment industry, whose high-fashion designers had thrived under Nancy Reagan's reign. The same fashion writers who during the campaign had lamented the demise of elegance, after the election gushed about the "new naturalness," frill-free, back-to-basics "investment dressing," and the American yearning to look "real."

During the campaign Barbara was overwhelmed by the amount of mail from people telling her "we love you" and don't worry about wrinkles or weight. "And they are all meant with great warmth and love," she explained to ABC's Barbara Walters, who interviewed the Bushes a few days before the inauguration.

"But they're saying something else," George hastened to add. "They're not talking about whether you're a blimp or not. What they are saying when they talk about Barbara is that they sense in her a certain genuineness. Her kids matter to her. Family is important to her. Ten years ago, they'd have hurt her feelings—and they don't."

She wasn't completely immune to what people said about her. "People can be so rude about the fact that George looks so young and I look so old," she sometimes said. "It's not nice." Friends said she suffered more than she ever let on. In August 1988, Cathleen Decker of the *Los Angeles Times* asked if she considered herself strong. "You lose your own image because people tell you all these horrible things," she replied. But she seemed never to let herself dwell on them. The temptation to poke fun at herself proved irresistible, even on national television. "George said to me, 'You don't want that dessert, do you? *Do* you?'" she told Barbara Walters. "And I said, 'Well, I have to eat it, George, for my fans.'"

She made self-deprecation an art. Joking about her white hair and her ample silhouette was a deliberate attempt to be funny, get a laugh, warm up a crowd, she told me during an early-1988 campaign trip in southern California. "People like to laugh a little," she said. "I think jokes about yourself are funnier than they are about other people." She acknowledged that she probably overdid it, but she didn't much care. It was a "defense, a wall," she admitted, but claimed she wouldn't be able to do it if she were insecure. "I know I'm very happy. I love my life."

She kept a mental gag bag filled with stories about herself that she could draw from for any occasion. She wrote about one of them in the "Campaign Diary": "I had a small crisis this week. I was staying at a very stylish hotel in New York City where I knew they always had a bathrobe in the closet, so I left mine at home. I had called room service for coffee, then discovered there was no robe. When the coffee came, I took a sheet off the bed and wrapped it around myself toga style to answer the door. I can just imagine what the waiter thought. I can just see him going back downstairs to the kitchen and saying, 'You'll never guess what I saw in room seventeen twelve!' "

That wasn't her only bathrobe story. Another was about the day Soviet Foreign Minister Eduard Shevardnadze was coming to breakfast at the Vice President's House, the thirty-three-room Victorian mansion off upper Massachusetts Avenue on the U.S. Naval Observatory grounds. It was six-thirty A.M., and Millie, Barbara's English springer spaniel, needed walking, so she slipped out of the house—only to hear a Secret Service agent cautioning that she might want to reconsider. Standing outside the fence—a telephoto lens away—was a battery of photographers, who would have been far more excited about a picture of the vice-president's wife in her bathrobe than one of Shevardnadze in his limousine. Barbara and Millie quickly changed direction, sneaking around the other side of the house. What she didn't know until she started to get dressed was that once Shevardnadze was inside the house, the press was repositioned on the front lawn, right under the big windows in the Bushes' dressing room. "I had to crawl to my closet to get my clothes," she said.

Her formal entertaining was gracious but unceremonious. A guest arriving at the Vice President's House for a black-tie dinner honoring Australian Prime Minister Robert J.L. Hawke in the spring of 1988 was surprised to see Millie, a tennis ball in her mouth, run into the living room. She dropped the ball and wagged her tail expectantly. Quipped Barbara, "I gave her a clean one in honor of the prime minister."

Despite official Washington's rigid adherence to protocol, Barbara adapted the rules of diplomatic precedence, the final authority by which ambassadors are ranked, laid down by the Congress of Vienna in 1815, to suit her needs. If she knew that a visiting foreign minister and the wife of the secretary of state had been to three successive dinners and seated next to each other at every one of them, she split them up at her house. And if the guest of honor's visit was brief, she didn't feel compelled to seat him at her table. "This poor man didn't come to the United States to sit next to me. So I'll try to put him at the table with

George so they can talk. I always make it clear that this is not the Vice President's idea, and they're very nice about it," she said.

She had married her own kind but never felt limited to them; she could take or leave the upper crust. "George and I aren't society," she once said, setting me straight on that score. "When have you ever seen us in *W*?" (the tony New York society biweekly).

Except for her literacy cause, and even then not all that frequently, she didn't solicit media coverage. In fact, as the Second Lady, she had avoided calling attention to herself, quite content that the spotlight play on Nancy Reagan and her anti-drug-abuse crusade. "Mrs. Bush was always incredibly courteous in making sure her staff worked with Mrs. Reagan's staff to avoid conflict," said Sheila Tate, Bush's campaign press secretary, who for four years had also been Nancy Reagan's press secretary. "I think she worked very hard at being a good vice-president's wife." Craig Fuller, George Bush's chief of staff for four years, saw her as "going out of her way to insure that the Reagans as President and First Lady were accorded the most favorable attention possible from this community, from the political environment."

Barbara didn't need compliments or ego massaging. But thinking she might nevertheless be pleased to hear it, Tate later told her what George had said about America's falling in love with Barbara Bush. Barbara just brushed Tate aside. She was like Bess Truman in that respect, a First Lady with whom

Barbara Bush and First Lady Nancy Reagan greet each other at the White House on January 11, 1989, shortly before the changing of the guard. This photo has been referred to around Washington as "The War of the Plaids." (*Courtesy Ronald Reagan Presidential Materials Project/Mary Anne Fackelman-Miner*)

Raisa Gorbachev, wife of Soviet Leader Mikhail Gorbachev, greets Barbara Bush at the Soviet Embassy on December 10, 1987, during the Washington Summit meeting. The Soviets indicated that Barbara was the preferred companion for Raisa, but the Reagan White House discouraged this, not wanting Nancy to be upstaged. (*David Valdez/The White House*)

The Reagans and the Bushes at the Vice President's House on February 13, 1981, one of the few times the two couples dined together privately over the eight years. In 1988, Barbara was infuriated by a *Time* magazine report that the Reagans never invited the Bushes to intimate dinners. (*Courtesy Ronald Reagan Presidential Materials Project/Mary Anne Fackelman-Miner*)

Barbara Bush applauds Nancy Reagan before her speech to the Congressional Club brunch at the Washington Shoreham Hotel on May 19, 1982. (*Lucian Perkins/Washington Post*)

Barbara Bush and Nancy Reagan join Marcela Perez de Cuellar, the wife of the UN Secretary General, in honoring Raisa Gorbachev at a luncheon on December 7, 1988. (*UN Photo 172540*)

Barbara packs for the twenty-ninth move in her forty-four-year marriage. "I'm a good mover-inner," quipped Barbara as she labeled boxes bound for the White House. "I'm just a bad mover-outer." While George dashed around town in those final days before taking office, Barbara complained lightheartedly that her husband was not helping one bit with the packing. (*David Valdez/ The White House*)

George and Barbara wave at the crowd as they walk in the inaugural parade on January 20, 1989. Barbara had stashed a second pair of shoes in the inaugural parade car, hoping security would allow them to walk part of the way. "People feel good at any inauguration, not just ours," Barbara noted. (*David Valdez/The White House*)

The Bushes at one of the nine inaugural balls. The First Lady is wearing a blue velvet and taffeta Arnold Scaasi gown. (*Michael Sargent/The White House*)

Formerly used as a beauty salon for First Ladies, Barbara had Nancy's hair dryers ripped out to make way for Millie's half-dozen puppies and other projects. Barbara and grandchild Marshall watch Millie take care of her litter. The puppies were born on March 17, 1989. (*David Valdez/The White House*)

Even as the nation's First Lady, Barbara vowed to lead a normal life. Barbara is the first person to walk her springer spaniel Millie each morning, typically crawling back into bed afterward to ease into the day with a cup of coffee. Here, she and Millie take a quiet stroll on the South Lawn. (*David Valdez/ The White House*)

The Bush brood gathers in the Yellow Oval Room to be photographed the day after the inauguration. The Bushes' ten grandchilden filled the White House with their laughter and toys, providing a sense of family that had been missing during the previous administration. Back row (*left to right*): Bill LeBlond, Doro Bush LeBlond, Neil Bush, Sharon Bush, Marshall Bush, Columba Bush, Marvin Bush (holding daughter Marshall), Jeb Bush, George Bush, Laura Bush. Children behind the President (*left to right*): Jenna and Barbara Bush, Noelle and George Bush. On the couch (*left to right*): Lauren and Pierce Bush, Barbara Bush, Jebby Bush, President George Bush, Ellie and Sam LeBlond, and Margaret Bush. (*David Valdez/The White House*)

Barbara at the Philadelphia Library on February 7, 1989, her debut out-of-town appearance as First Lady. Barbara, coming from a family of "omnivorous readers," chose literacy as her cause. Her son Neil triumphed over his dyslexia because his mother fought the disability early on with a battery of tutors and extensive testing. (*Carol T. Powers/The White House*)

The First Lady, in the second week in her new role, reads to children at Martha's Table, a Washington soup kitchen. "Reading disability isn't a class thing, it isn't racial, it happens to anybody. Unless a parent is supportive, well-prepared, and recognizes the problem, a child can be lost forever," says Barbara's son Neil. (*Carol T. Powers/The White House*)

Barbara holds a baby March 22, 1989, at Grandma's House, a Washington facility for babies with AIDS. (*Carol T. Powers/The White House*)

Barbara is feted by The National Literacy Honors on November 15, 1988, in Washington. (*David Valdez/The White House*)

Two weeks after their Canadian trip, the Bushes fly to the Far East for a three-nation tour. The First Lady admires an elephant statue in Beijing's Forbidden City. (*Carol T. Powers/The White House*)

Mila Mulroney, wife of Canadian Prime Minister Brian Mulroney, shows Barbara around the National Gallery of Canada on February 10, 1989. The night before the Bushes arrived in Canada, the President had revealed his plans for a $2.5 billion initiative to deal with acid rain caused by U.S. industrial emissions. (*Carol T. Powers/The White House*)

The Bushes give a dinner in Beijing in honor of President Yang Shangkur (standing between the President and Mrs. Bush). Texas-style barbecue is served and American flags decorate the floral arrangements. Since George's post as Chief of the Liaison Office in China in 1974–75, the couple had returned several times to visit. But this trip was special, both as a sentimental journey and a symbol of an expanding relationship between the two nations. (*David Valdez/The White House*)

George and Barbara on February 24, 1989, in Tokyo, attending the funeral of Japanese Emperor Hirohito. (*Carol T. Powers/The White House*)

she was sometimes compared. It was a characteristic only too familiar to her family. When praised, "she's liable to say, 'Oh, cut it out,' " said George's sister, Nancy Ellis, who had known Barbara since they were teenagers.

Discomfited by campaign questions about what kind of First Lady she would be, Barbara at one point complained, "I wish they'd quit asking me that." But she seemed reconciled to becoming a role model by the time the inauguration rolled around, though she admonished reporters not to compare her to Eleanor Roosevelt. "I grew up in a household that really detested her," she said in a group interview at the Vice President's House, going on to explain that her mother "really didn't like" Mrs. Roosevelt, although she later softened up a bit after meeting her at the White House. "So let's talk about someone else," said Barbara. Sounding almost wistful, she said of her own view of herself: "I still look in the mirror and see a young sixteen-year-old whose tennis game could improve. But that isn't the way it is really."

And the way it was really?

"I'll tell you," she said, brightening, "my mail tells me a lot of fat, white-haired, wrinkled ladies are tickled pink."

After eight years in Nancy Reagan's shadow and after a flawless performance as a loyal Second Lady who never forgot her place, Barbara Bush was acknowledging her impact. Other than being devoted to their husbands, she and Nancy really had little in common. At its best, their relationship was courteous, at its worst, remote. "I was always grateful that Nancy and I could be very good friends and didn't have to do stuff together all the time," she said. Then, realizing how she had put it, she clarified herself. "I don't mean that quite the way it sounds. I mean I had interests of my own that I wanted to do, so I didn't feel I had to run around and be a lady-in-waiting. It was just a nice feeling."

Physical differences aside, to the media Nancy appeared to be aloof, cool, and ungiving in relationships, Barbara welcoming and companionable. Nancy kept her family at arm's length; Barbara enveloped hers. Nancy was seen as a creature of Rodeo Drive luxury; Barbara of Down East necessity. Nancy often used others, behind the scenes, to influence her husband; Barbara worked directly and through example.

The media's urge to compare the two always bothered Barbara. "I hate it, because first of all, I lose on that particular comparison," she said. "But she and I are not alike and you can't compare apples and oranges, or whatever. And that doesn't take away from my enormous respect for her, and the job she's doing. So I hate that, the comparisons I read."

What she hated more were the parallels drawn of the Reagans and the Bushes, their backgrounds, their lifestyles, their families, their friends. Aides said she had tried to tone down the contrasts that last week before inauguration day, when she and Nancy had to share the national spotlight. But to outsiders it appeared just the opposite. Nobody at an inaugural tribute to her at the Kennedy Center, for instance, would have guessed it. Giving her "Bush Blue" Arnold Scaasi jacket a tug and striking a model's pose, she provided 6,000 gleeful fans a glimpse of what Marilyn Quayle, who introduced her, called her "wicked wit." "Speaking of glamour," said Barbara, not once but three times as she visited each of the Center's big halls, "I want you all to look at me. Please notice—hairdo, makeup, designer dress. Look at me good this week, because it's the only week." The message—that she and Nancy Reagan were different women with vastly different values—was unmistakable.

There had been whispers about the relationship between the Reagans and the Bushes throughout Reagan's two terms. And Washington, which kept track of such things with more than casual interest, read meaning into everything. In November 1985, when Nancy Reagan drew up her guest list from New York and Hollywood glitterati for the exclusive dinner she and the president gave for Britain's Prince Charles and Princess Diana, some in town suspected it was a snub to the Bushes, who were seen out on their own that night at the National Theatre just two blocks away. The Bushes were given their chance to dine with the royals the next night at the British Embassy, which rounded up a more typical example of Washington nightlife by inviting high-ranking—if unglamorous—administration officials.

The snub that Washington missed came in December 1987 during the Washington summit meeting of Ronald Reagan and Soviet leader Mikhail Gorbachev. Because of the chilly interaction between Nancy Reagan and Raisa Gorbachev at the 1985 Geneva summit, the Soviet Embassy had welcomed any opportunity for Raisa to be with Barbara. The two women had first met in Moscow in 1985 when the Bushes attended the funeral of Gorbachev's predecessor, Konstantin Chernenko; at a breakfast Bush hosted for Gorbachev, Barbara and Raisa found they had a mutual interest in education and from all reports, seemed to get along fine. But for the Washington summit, the White House was calling the shots, and the Bushes were looked upon as relatively minor players. After the Soviet Embassy indicated a preference for Barbara Bush to accompany Raisa Gorbachev to the National Gallery of Art, Bush's office got the word back from the White House: "That was not to be encouraged," Craig Fuller remembered. "It was made clear that this would not be looked upon favorably." Other than moments in receiving lines— at a White House dinner and a Soviet Embassy breakfast—and seeing the Gorbachevs off at Andrews Air Force Base, Barbara was given no costarring role with Raisa.

As spring 1988 dragged on and Ronald Reagan still had not announced his support of Bush for the GOP presidential nomination, stories circulated that Nancy was the problem. *Time* magazine reported that she had forced the cancellation of an appearance by her husband at a Bush rally a short distance from the White House because "she did not have much affection or trust for Bush"—a report both Reagan and Bush aides denied.

In the same report, *Time* wrote that Nancy had refused to attend a star-studded Bush rally in Los Angeles even though she was staying at the same hotel. What it did not report was that some Reagan aides worked behind the scenes to suggest that Barbara Bush shouldn't attend either. "That never came to me directly, though I later heard there was such talk," confirmed Craig Fuller. "I really left it up to Mrs. Bush and the Vice President as to what they wanted to do, and she wanted to be there. So I called back and said Mrs. Bush was coming."

What infuriated Barbara in the *Time* story was a sentiment "friends" attributed to her that Nancy was "strikingly ungrateful for all the loyalty and deference the Bushes have shown the Reagans for eight years," and in an interview with me that fall she said that she had called Nancy, then told George to write her a note to counter the report. "I said, 'We are not going to let a mischievous, dumb, unfunny, untrue story upset a close friendship—we're not going to do it. The so-called friends are made up. I never said anything like that.' " What had made her laugh, she said, was to read in the same story that the Reagans never invited the Bushes to "intimate" dinners. "George said to me, 'You know, that reminds me, we haven't had the Reagans over for dinner in years. You think we ought to ask them?' " The Bushes did have the Reagans over in 1981, but subsequent exchanges of dinners were few and far between.

But "intimate" the Bushes and Reagans decidedly were not. The way the Bushes really relaxed was with "those one or two people, close friends, you really really know"—the ones they could call up at the last minute and ask over or go out with for dinner. "I would expect the Reagans to do the same thing," Barbara said, although in their eight years in Washington the Reagans rarely made spur-of-the-moment outings to local restaurants as the Bushes routinely did.

A loyalist like George, Barbara offered a noble public defense of Nancy when questioned by the media. "I'm not sure a lot of that wasn't fiction," she said of stories about Nancy's behind-the-scenes influence on her husband's White House staff. In January 1989, as Barbara prepared to move to 1600 Pennsylvania Avenue, she called the upstairs of the White House "sparkling" and said Americans should have said thank-you for the new White House china, though she also mused that it would probably have been better for Nancy had she replaced it piece by piece.

So that Nancy Reagan could redecorate her living quarters at the White House, Reagan friends had raised more than $1 million in tax-deductible contributions in 1981, prompting a public outcry. The contributions included $209,000 worth of White House china. But "they also fixed the plumbing, the electricity. I'm in her debt," said Barbara. Like Nancy, she believed in raising money privately to beautify her government housing; the Bushes' friends had raised $187,000 in 1981 to spruce up the Vice President's House. Their largesse, however, had gone virtually unnoticed, as had the hundreds of parties the Bushes gave at taxpayer expense in what she called a Washington "safe house"—meaning no press.

Even Barbara Bush admitted it was unusual. Of her eight years as the Second Lady she said shortly before George became president: "I got away with murder."

2

The Honeymooners

"I'm not really sure I am the First Lady of the land, but I like being married to the President."

*E*normous goodwill awaited the Bushes in Washington that January. George Bush was a charter member of the elite Eastern Establishment and a twenty-three-year veteran of its capital branch, whose partisan movers and shakers might come and go but whose influence had not wavered in two centuries. Barbara Bush's credentials were equally impeccable. She was a favorite in mainstream Republican circles and respected at opposite ends of the party spectrum as well. As a couple, the Bushes were the ultimate insiders, sociable and self-assured and endowed with manners, connections, pedigree, and an unquestioned commitment to public service.

In that giddy way Washington behaves when a new president takes office, the city handed Bush a honeymoon even before he repeated his vows. Rough times would come, but for now, after a long, acrimonious campaign, both Democrats and Republicans were talking optimistically of a resurrected bipartisanship, of forging a workable partnership to carry on the nation's business.

Barbara Bush was seen as a refreshing new presence in the White House. Her loyalties were well-certified and her friends—from both parties—legion. "I can't live without them," she said, quite willing to name the "forty-nine closest friends" she could call on at the drop of a hat were it not for the "burden" such attention would put upon them. She was as familiar with Capitol Hill, where as wife of the Vice President she had led the Senate Ladies for eight years, as she was with Embassy Row, where her connections went back to Bush's service as U.S. ambassador to the United Nations from 1971 to 1973 and Chief of the U.S. Liaison Office in China in 1974–75, as well as to his vice-presidential globe-trotting days. Like the affable Bush, she also had worked at her friendships, keeping up with women she knew from George's days as a congressman and as an appointee in the Nixon and Ford administrations.

By mid-January, with the inauguration only days away, the time had come for Barbara to claim the spotlight and begin to share with her public what she thought about moving into 1600 Pennsylvania Avenue and becoming America's thirty-eighth First Lady.

In one of a series of sessions with the media, she invited a half-dozen newspaper reporters to the Vice President's House, where she was as chatty as a back-fence neighbor. "Feeling silly," though clearly in her element, she sat with us at the dining room table, talked about the packing, and good-naturedly groused about this twenty-ninth move in her forty-four-year marriage. "I'm a good mover-inner," she quipped. "I'm just a bad mover-outer." Little red dots were stuck on everything destined for the living room at the White House; she joked that some dots might be on art works that didn't belong to the Bushes but were on loan to the Vice President's House. "If we don't end up with a museum piece at the White House that isn't ours, and our junk at the museums, I'll be surprised," she said, laughing.

Already Barbara was finding out about the price of fame. A year earlier, she had vowed that no matter who won the presidency, Millie was going to have puppies in 1989. Now, out of town on her own honeymoon and not due back until after Inauguration Day, Millie was the wag of Washington. "I mean, Millie made the front page of the paper when I casually said she was getting married," Barbara said, citing that as a good example of how the life she had loved as Second Lady—"I never felt besieged"—would change.

The night before, the Reagans had had the Bushes over to the White House for dinner, and a few days earlier Nancy had taken Barbara on a tour of the upstairs family quarters. Included in Nancy's parting advice had been one provocative piece. "She did advise me not to have my children live in the White House—for whatever that's worth," Barbara told another group of reporters weeks later. "I told her I hadn't invited them."

Her immediate concern was the practical side of living in the White House. Barbara and Paola Rendon, the Bushes' housekeeper for thirty years, had wondered about that since the election. One question was whether a washer and dryer were on the premises. "There are three of each," announced Barbara. "She'll just have those running all the time. I said to Paola, 'You're going to be in heaven.' "

With Nancy leading the way, Barbara had also checked out White House sleeping accommodations. Her organizational talents were apparent as she outlined the room assignments she had made for the inaugural weekend. Marvin and Margaret Bush would sleep in the supposedly haunted Lincoln Bedroom, where King George VI had slept during his and Queen Elizabeth's 1939 state visit; the other four Bush children, their spouses, and offspring in other choice bedrooms. The Queen's Bedroom, so named because the queen slept there on that same visit, would go to Dorothy Walker Bush, George's eighty-seven-year-old mother, the unquestioned matriarch of the Bush clan. Though in poor health, Dorothy Bush had wanted to see her son inaugurated, to be a part of things as she always had been, and to do it she traveled to and from Florida by ambulance plane, accompanied by a doctor and a nurse. "She looked tiny in that great bed," Barbara remembered later.

In those final heady days before he would take the presidential oath, George Bush had seemed in perpetual motion, dashing around Washington, going out to dinner, buying new clothes—but not helping out one bit with the packing, Barbara complained. If the immensity of the tasks ahead bothered him, Barbara saw no signs of it. "I think he's a very put-together person," she said, sharing a glimpse of his deadpan sense of humor. Why, only that day she had asked him how his inaugural speech was coming along because "people are always asking me."

"What speech?" George asked.

"God, George," she replied, "you got a big speech coming!"

When January 20 finally arrived, Barbara woke up early, the day organized in her mind. But there was a problem. Her eyes, which had been bothering her, were red and puffy. She would learn a few days later that it was because her thyroid gland was producing excess levels of thyroid hormone. But that morning she had no idea. "I thought my handlers had gotten makeup in them," she said. "I said, 'Listen, my eyes have closed and you all have ruined me. Don't do any eye makeup.' "

The Bushes, surrounded by children and grandchildren in various stages of mounting excitement, were staying at Blair House, the President's official guesthouse across Pennsylvania Avenue from the

White House. Strewn about the elegant sitting rooms, usually filled with the trappings of kings and presidents, were the impedimenta of small children— stuffed toys, coloring books, computer games. "I'll tell you," said Nancy Ellis, who joined her brother and sister-in-law for coffee before everybody trekked across Lafayette Square for a morning service at St. John's Church, "those curators looked mighty nervous."

At noon, standing on the windswept west front of the Capitol, with Barbara at his side holding the same Bible George Washington had used two hundred years earlier, George Herbert Walker Bush repeated the oath of office as the nation's forty-first president. Meeting on "democracy's front porch," talking as if to neighbors and friends, he spoke of "high moral principle" and making "kinder the face of the nation and gentler the face of the world."

"There are the homeless, lost and roaming. There are the children who have nothing, no love, no normalcy. There are those who cannot free themselves of enslavement to whatever addiction—drugs, welfare, demoralization that rules the slums," he said. "There is crime to be conquered, the rough crime of the streets. There are young women to be helped who are about to become mothers of children they can't care for and might not love. They need our care, our guidance, and education; though we bless them for choosing life."

As she listened, Barbara knew that not everyone would like his mentioning some of those problems.

"But I was glad he remembered," she said. "You know, it's hard to run the world vis-à-vis the Russians and trying to solve enormous disasters like an oil spill, and I remember thinking it was wonderful that he mentioned them. . . . He could have left out some of those social issues, but he put them all in."

There would be "hard choices," the president continued, "looking at what we have and perhaps allocating it differently, making our decisions based on honest need and prudent safety. And then we will do the wisest thing of all. We will turn to the only resource we have that in times of need always grows: the goodness and the courage of the American people."

Later, Barbara couldn't recall everything that went on in her mind during the speech, but she did remember that even though many thought the kinder, gentler side George was showing was due to her, she didn't feel proprietary. "No, because one thing I learned in married life, you don't really advise. By osmosis things sometimes work. So I felt very good about his speech. He talked about the things, the issues important to me."

After he finished, the Bushes got in the inaugural-parade car, where Barbara had stashed a second pair of shoes. They'd gotten Secret Service permission to walk part of the way if they did it "spontaneously." "George said, 'I want to walk as much as we can,' so they let us out when they thought it was safe. Security was of major importance," Barbara remembered. "We walked maybe three times, five minutes—not enough. You know, it's so frustrating riding in a car that's going two miles an hour. You know you can walk faster than that."

Everyone seemed buoyant. "People feel good at any inauguration, not just ours," Barbara said, even mentioning the feeling at the inauguration of Democrat Jimmy Carter twelve years earlier. "People feel good about their country, about a change of leadership. I don't know if it's because we're so secure that we don't feel threatened or that people love the people who've been elected. But anyway, there was a feeling of just a great day."

Two sets of moving vans—one bringing the Bushes' belongings to the mansion, the other carrying the Reagans' things out—had been lined up in the White House driveway that morning at the very moment Nancy and Ronald Reagan looked down from the presidential helicopter during one last flyover before heading out to Andrews Air Force Base. By the time George and Barbara got to the White House, their belongings were already in place, and the Reagans' things on their way to California.

All afternoon as the inaugural parade passed by, none of the Bushes could get used to the idea that when Barbara said "the house," she meant the White House behind them. When son Neil Bush and his daughter Lauren went inside for something to drink, a White House usher offered to show them around. It had been some time since children had the run of the White House. The man operating the elevator looked at Lauren, who was four, then asked if she knew whose elevator it was. She did not, of course, since she had never ridden it before. "This is the President's elevator," he explained, adding gently but firmly lest the rules be broken: "And we don't yell on the President's elevator."

That night everybody went to the inaugural balls. George had never been much of a dancer, even though Barbara always insisted he was and that he only said he wasn't because he "really didn't love it." Dancing at these parties, though, was a necessary evil—"That's show business," George said—and he had resigned himself. At their first stop, at Union Station, the band played "I Could Have Danced All Night." George clearly didn't feel up to that. He grumbled to the 5,000 ballgoers, "You can say you saw it first here, a lousy dancer trying to dance his first dance with the First Lady of the United States of America."

Her first family breakfast in the White House Saturday morning wasn't quite what Barbara had expected. "Some of those children of ours had danced till three or four in the morning," Barbara said. It took a while for everybody to get dressed and into the Yellow Oval Room so White House photographer David Valdez could take the official family photo. Meanwhile, "the grandchildren, and there were ten in the house, came in and climbed on our bed and played. And we did have a wonderful time," she said. After breakfast, they went to the North Portico to greet some of the 30,000 people lined up outside to pay their respects. When Marvin Bush, their youngest son, saw that crowd, he knew he was home. As long as he could remember, his parents' house had been a place people liked to visit.

Dorothy Bush, upstairs with her doctor and nurse, watched through a Queen's Bedroom window. "People were waving at her and she was waving, and Jenna [Bush, a granddaughter] and I walked up to stand by, and people waved at us," Barbara said. "People recognized my hair and said, 'Come on out'—you know, gesturing. And we said, 'We can't, we can't.' And out of the blue about eighty people who did not know each other burst into 'God Bless America.' So we stood at full attention, with little Mrs. Bush—the doctor, the nurse, Jenna, and I—we stood at full attention while they finished. It was so sweet. It was such a nice moment, and I think probably the nicest moment of the inauguration."

At one point later in the day, Barbara looked out the window again. "And there on the driveway was George Bush's mother in the wheelchair, with her doctor, and she was shaking hands and greeting people as they came out the front doorstep. How she got there I don't know."

By Monday, Dorothy Bush and George and Barbara's offspring had cleared out, leaving behind teddy bears, stray socks, and a lingering sense of family that had been missing in the Reagan White House. It was Bush's first working day as president, and it began with an early-morning ceremony at which Vice President Dan Quayle administered the oath of office to the new White House team.

With Barbara looking on, George warned that the staff could expect to work long hours in jobs known to be "time-consuming" killers, but that their efforts "could result in a country with more opportunity for all. . . . The lights burn brightly, well after dark around this place, and I just hope you'll be understanding because the system works that way—work is never done." Barbara Bush understood that, he said. "She's set a good example, it seems to me, in a lot of volunteer action," and since government couldn't do it all, he was encouraging the volunteer sector—"the 'thousand points of light' that I plan to keep on talking about"—to get involved.

That night after dinner, alone for the first time as President and First Lady, the Bushes went exploring with the zest of any couple moving into their dream house. Barbara had to pinch herself sometimes. How could anybody not be thrilled by the view of the Washington Monument, by being able to choose which of the forty-president collection of White House china to eat from each day—"I ate off Grover Cleveland at lunch today. I had Abraham Lincoln yesterday. Can you believe that?"—by living amid such beauty and history? "If you couldn't be happy in the White House, you just couldn't be happy anywhere," she said.

She was an eager tour guide, showing her staff and friends Abraham Lincoln's only signed copy of the Gettysburg address in the Lincoln Bedroom, pointing out a false wall concealing a secret staircase. She did as she pleased—startling, then delighting

White House tour-goers in the driveway below by waving good-bye from the window of the Queen's Bedroom. She found that she could also wave at George from her upstairs office on the southwest corner if he happened to glance up from his Oval Office desk in the West Wing. Her own great-great-great-uncle President Franklin Pierce had had his office in The Treaty Room, also known as the Monroe Room, and it was there the Bushes decided George should have his home office.

She saw no need to redecorate, only to incorporate what the Bushes had brought with them. Among her less publicized changes was taking out Nancy Reagan's hair dryers to make way for Millie's puppies and the five dozen family scrapbooks—"the essence of our life"—so she had elbow room to work on them. She turned her attention to Camp David, the Catoctin Mountain retreat for every president since Franklin D. Roosevelt, inviting New York interior designer Mark Hampton, her decorator in 1981 at the Vice President's House, to survey its needs.

The 250 Bush and Pierce relatives she and George had invited to lunch that inaugural Saturday had been just the beginning. Before long a marathon of private dinners was in progress upstairs at the White House, some put together the same day. After George invited twenty in for dinner the same night—forty were already invited the following night—word got around that the chef was threatening to quit. Talking later about the increased work load, Barbara said she told the staff she hoped they weren't overburdened but she had "very bad news. I think you might just as well accept it. We did this at the Vice President's House, and we're going to do it—I know he is—so we've got to accommodate."

Despite what George Bush led everybody to think, Barbara Bush had no intention of serving pork rinds at White House parties. "I wish George had never said he liked them," she complained of the "caseloads" of pork rinds people sent. What's more, barbecue had its place—and the Bushes had served their share through the years, and would again soon on a trip to China—but not at black-tie functions, which were the kind she thought George and she should give as America's official hosts.

Not since Carter and his brood had there been such a large and close-knit clan coming and going at the White House. Nevertheless, some things would be different. At two of Carter's official dinners, daughter Amy read a book at the table. Barbara didn't want to "get personal," she told United Press International's Iris Krasnow, "but I am one who honestly isn't going to have grandchildren coming to dinners. I just think that's not right."

Appropriately, the Bushes' first big official White House party was an elegant buffet for 160 chiefs of foreign missions in Washington's diplomatic corps. Barbara wore her designer inaugural-ball gown that night, a blue velvet and taffeta Arnold Scaasi original. Bush came in white tie, but without his voice, having lost it to laryngitis. "I told him, 'Don't talk—I can read your lips,' " the ambassador of Mauritius advised him as he went through the receiving line, a teasing reminder of Bush's campaign buzz phrase about not raising taxes.

Barbara had vowed to live a normal life. "I'm going to get out a lot. I'm going to museums. I'm going to walk. I'm going to go with friends. I'm just going to do things because I think there's a danger of being trapped in the White House," she said. "I mean, look at how pretty it is. Who'd want to leave it?" So she dropped in at the National Gallery of Art to see the Paul Cézanne exhibit and walked her dog along Pennsylvania Avenue. And before a month had passed, she threw the switch, as it were, for Bush's "thousand points of light."

She chose Philadelphia as the city to kick off her literacy crusade, careful to draw a distinction between her status as volunteer and that of activist. "I don't feel my job is to do the senator's job," she said of Republican Pennsylvania senator Arlen Specter, who was in her entourage, when asked about government programs aimed at job training and maternal literacy. "Or the president's job," she added. "I feel my job is to encourage the corporate and private sector to help, whether it's individuals or agencies or Rotary Clubs or Lions Clubs."

Around Washington, she did what she had been doing quietly for years, dropping in on groups that help the less fortunate. She put on an apron to make sandwiches for a mobile soup kitchen supplied by an eight-year-old nonprofit group called Martha's Table. Cleaning out her closet, she took her old clothes to a thrift shop where they could be sold at prices the less-advantaged could afford. She took valentines to elderly friends at The Washington Home for Incurables. She sang from memory all six verses of "We Shall Overcome" at a Black History Month school assembly that the Washington Parent Group Fund, a favorite enrichment program for needy schools, helped arrange. She postponed a trip to New York in order to be at Andrews Air Force Base when a mercy flight arranged by Project Hope touched down with thirty-seven victims of the December 7 earthquake in Soviet Armenia. It had seemed "sort of fitting," she explained, since her son John Ellis (Jeb) Bush and his son George Prescott had flown there the previous December as goodwill envoys.

She attracted media attention wherever she went. Newspapers and television contributed to the hope of many Americans that the homeless, the needy, the elderly, and the working poor had an advocate at last in the White House. By late February, as George Bush was drawing criticism because he appeared to be stalled in organizing his administration, vague in deciding his long-term goals, and headed for a politically bloody showdown over former Texas senator John Tower's nomination as secretary of defense, Barbara Bush was having quite the opposite effect on Washington's highly vocal political observers. Her popularity was rising fast.

"The honeymoon is still on," she replied when asked how it felt being "the First Lady of the land." "I'm not really sure I am the First Lady of the land, but I like being married to the President and I love my life. So I feel pretty good."

The most widely traveled of any American president's wife by the time she reached the White House, she had accompanied Bush to sixty-eight countries and four territories when he was vice president, on trips totaling 1,330,239 miles—the equivalent of fifty-four times around the world. There was hardly a world leader she hadn't met. "Not that they know me, but I know them," she joked. Virtually unnoticed by the media on those journeys abroad, she had enjoyed her anonymity.

That, too, had changed. In early February, when she went to Canada with Bush on his first trip abroad as president, she was met by a media more interested in her views on acid rain than her concerns about people who couldn't read. Having reported the comings and goings of Nancy Reagan for eight years, the members of the Canadian press were curious about this woman who refused to dye her white hair, go on a diet, or accept designer clothes as free loans. They seemed confused about her. Two French-speaking reporters observing her and Mila Mulroney, wife of Canada's prime minister, reading to school children in Ottawa debated from the sidelines whether Barbara was trying to make America "more liberal" or "more literal." But an English-speaking correspondent for the *Globe and Mail* had it right. Noting that neither woman had finished college, he sighed. "We've got two college dropouts, both pushing literacy," he said, then added wryly, "But they both married well."

Bush's budget message to the U.S. Congress the night before his trip had revealed his plans for a $2.5 billion initiative dealing with acid rain caused by U.S. industrial emissions. On official levels, there seemed to be reason for optimism among the Americans and Canadians, but reporters trailing Barbara around the National Gallery of Canada were skeptical. Did she realize that some of the lakes reproduced in the paintings she was looking at and calling "beautiful" were dead from acid rain? As if she had not heard the question, she replied, "They're beautiful." No one saw it then, but in retrospect her response seemed like the first indication of a retreat that would be complete before the end of the month.

Two weeks later the Bushes flew to the Far East on a three-nation trip that began with the funeral of Emperor Hirohito in Tokyo. Memories weren't so short and World War II wasn't so long ago that Bush's decision to attend hadn't come under some criticism at home. On American television, panels debated how he, a WWII torpedo bomber pilot who was the only survivor when he and his two crewmen were shot down by the Japanese, could pay respects to a man responsible for the deaths of thousands of young Americans. Barbara was nineteen and engaged to George then. If anybody had told her that forty-five years later she would be representing the United States at Hirohito's funeral, she would never have believed it. "To us, Hirohito was a villain, I mean the worst," she told me in May 1989. "Then George and I met him several years ago and he was beguiling—a tiny, sweet, gentle, charming man and lovely host."

Some Japanese had privately criticized George for arranging bilateral talks with other foreign leaders during a time of national mourning, but the Japanese government welcomed Bush's selection of Japan as the first Far East country he would visit as president. In order to seat Bush in the principal mourners' tent, palace protocol officials scurried to get around traditional order of precedence, which is based on the date a king, president, or prime minister took office. The Solomon-like solution was that guests whose country Hirohito had visited and guests he had met outranked everyone else. Bush scored high on both counts; Hirohito came to the United States in October 1975, and Bush, as vice president, had met him in 1982 in Tokyo. A favorite photograph of that meeting, part of Barbara's campaign slide show, always brought a chuckle when she passed it at the Vice President's House. It showed the diminutive Hirohito standing with the Bushes—"Papa Bear, Mama Bear, and Baby Bear," she joked to audiences.

The funeral trip gave Bush a chance to try to shore up Japanese-American relations against the ongoing and still touchy trade differences between the two countries. Barbara, an old hand at diplomatic tiptoeing, had been adamant about keeping a low profile during the brief stay and had refused interview requests by the Japanese media. She had kept her own Tokyo schedule secret until the day before she and Bush left Washington. When released, it consisted of nothing more public than two teas on successive days, one with the wife of the Japanese foreign minister and the other with the wife of Mexico's new president, who was also at the funeral. In private, she dined at her hotel with a small group of Japanese women, among them the daughter of Japan's wartime foreign minister, Ise Togo, whose husband once was Japan's ambassador to Washington. By George Bush's side at the funeral, Barbara was a serene and elegant figure in black, betraying none of her girlhood emotions.

The trip to China that followed was quite another story. Bush had returned four times since he was Liaison Chief there, and Barbara had been back five. But this first visit as President and First Lady was special, both a sentimental journey and a symbol of what Bush called an "expanding relationship" between the two countries since the Shanghai Communiqué was signed in February 1972.

Bush gave handmade cowboy boots with American and Chinese flags on them to his hosts, who received them with slight disdain. "In our country we don't have the habit of putting flags on boots," Chinese premier Li Peng told him. "In our country we don't have that habit either," Bush replied readily. Nothing seemed to put a damper on his mood. "One generation plants a tree, the next sits in its shade," Bush said, quoting a Chinese proverb during a welcoming dinner in Beijing's Great Hall of the People. It was a night to be expansive, to "keep planting trees." Bush commended the Chinese leaders' "courageous reforms" that made it possible for "the people of China [to] have more opportunities to express themselves and to make important decisions in their personal and professional lives," a reference that would seem ironic only twenty-four hours later. When the Bushes entertained their hosts with a Texas-style barbecue at a reciprocal dinner the next night, Chinese authorities denied entry to one prominent invited guest, Chinese astrophysicist Fang Lizhi, an outspoken critic of China's communist system. Barbara said later she had been unaware of the incident that night. Like the rest of the world, she learned the next day just how angry the Chinese leaders were when they publicly protested to the U.S. for our having invited a leading dissident to the dinner. Three months later, those Chinese "reforms" Bush had spoken of so optimistically would seem a sham when hundreds were killed as government troops moved on protesters in Beijing and the country appeared to be on the brink of civil war. And Fang, accused of helping to incite the student uprising that sparked the attack, would be given refuge in the American embassy.

At the time, though, nothing so grim seemed on the horizon. Like any tourists with fond memories of a place, the Bushes spent much of their two-day stay reminiscing about the thirteen months they had lived in China. Barbara was a lively companion riding in from the airport with Bette Bao Lord, whose husband, Winston, was then the American ambassador. Dusting off her Chinese, Barbara recalled one recitation in particular: "No, it's not a cat. Yes, it's a dog.

No, it doesn't bite." She used to repeat it when walking Millie's predecessor, C. Fred, the Bushes' cocker spaniel, because the Chinese, preferring their dog on the dinner plate, had found C. Fred an appetizing curiosity.

"Today we came up with twenty motorcars in a motorcade, and I used to come to church on my bicycle—my Flying Pigeon," Bush told the congregation at the Beijing Chongmenwen Christian Church, where their youngest child, Dorothy, had been baptized. Barbara also traveled by motorcade, and at the Forbidden City, once the home of China's emperors and a favorite haunt during her thirteen months there, she, too, was struck by the change in her status. She remembered how she would ride her bicycle there from the American Embassy and give someone two cents to park it while she and a houseguest spent the afternoon touring the 250-acre museum. The Forbidden City hadn't changed—except that "you weren't here," she pointedly told her media escorts.

That event, too, was flawed. In the Hall of Supreme Harmony, Chinese security guards shoved a slender young American woman named Carol Powers, the White House photographer assigned to cover Barbara, into a doorway. The force of impact dislocated Powers's jaw. Barbara wasn't yet aware of that when she complained to Yang Xin, the museum's director, "This girl's job is to take my picture, and she got hit. She works for my husband. Ask them to calm down."

Nancy Reagan's foreign trips had been preceded by as many as three waves of staffers planning her appearances. Barbara had recoiled from such elaborate and costly arrangements, believing the embassies could handle those details, as the U.S. Mission had when President and Betty Ford visited China in December 1975. Barbara ordered home one White House aide when she found out the woman was en route to the Far East to advance her trip. Clearly annoyed by the commotion surrounding her visit, Barbara was curt later when a reporter raised questions about the inadequate press arrangements: "You're just saying that to be rude because you know I don't want to be advanced," she told Craig Hind of the *Houston Chronicle*, giving reporters a glimpse of her testiness with the press as she brushed the question aside.

The trip snafus, the criticism of Bush, and Barbara's irritation were all evidence that the honeymoon was ending, as they all do. Back home there was bigger trouble. In an early February interview, the Associated Press had quoted Barbara as saying she thought military assault rifles of the type that had been used in the schoolyard killings of five California children should be outlawed—"absolutely." It was an offhand remark rooted in heartfelt emotion, but it was at odds with the gun control policy then being pushed by Bush, a member and ardent supporter of the National Rifle Association, and it touched off a flap that quickly spread to Capitol Hill.

Ever since she had made the remark, White House aides wondered when the next shoe would fall.

Barbara Pierce, age seven, in Rye, New York. (*Bush Family Album*)

The Pierce family in 1928. *Left to right*: Her brother James, her mother, Pauline Pierce, her father, Marvin Pierce, Barbara in her father's lap, and her sister, Martha. (*Courtesy Scott Pierce*)

Barbara (*far right*) taking a walk with her friend Joan Herman (plaid coat) and the ever-present menagerie, in Indian Village (Rye, New York). (*Courtesy Rosanne Morgan Clarke*)

Growing up in Rye, New York, Barbara and her friends pretend they are statues in an empty fountain. *Left to right*: Barbara, Rosanne "Posy" Morgan, Kate Siedle. (*Courtesy Rosanne Morgan Clarke*)

Barbara and her friends slide down a wall. *Top to bottom*: Kate Siedle, June Biedler, and Barbara. (*Courtesy Rosanne Morgan Clarke*)

Clowning around, the girls lounge in an empty fountain in June Biedler's backyard. *Left to right*: Rosanne "Posy" Morgan, June Biedler, Barbara. (*Courtesy Rosanne Morgan Clarke*)

Barbara as Beatrice (*far left*) in an Ashley Hall production of *Much Ado About Nothing* in 1942. (*Courtesy Ashley Hall*)

Barbara's Ashley Hall graduation picture, 1943. (*Courtesy Cordelia Lambert Stites*)

Barbara (*second from right*) runs with schoolmates on Ashley Hall's athletic field in her junior year. (*Ashley Hall 1942 yearbook/Courtesy Cordelia Lambert Stites*)

Barbara and George in Texas, summer of 1948. *(Bush Family Album)*

During Barbara and George's courtship, George asked Pauline Pierce for a photo of her daughter. This is the one she gave him of Barbara, with her dog Sandy. *(Courtesy Rosanne Morgan Clarke)*

George and Barbara dance at their wedding January 6, 1945. Forty-four years later, they're still dancing. George claims that he isn't much of a dancer, but has acknowledged that "that's show business." (*Bush Family Album*)

Barbara, on her wedding day, is surrounded by her family (Marvin Pierce, *far left*, Pauline Pierce, *far right*). (*Bush Family Album*)

Meet the newlyweds: Lt. (jg) and Mrs. George Herbert Walker Bush. (*Bush Family Album*)

The Pierce bunch at home in Rye, New York, in the mid-forties. (*Left to right*: Barbara, her sister, Martha, Martha's one-year-old daughter, Sharon, an unidentified family friend, Barbara's brothers, Scott and James (in sailor suit). (*Bush Family Album*)

Barbara and George at Yale, after George leaves the Navy. (*Bush Family Album*)

In George and Barbara's New Haven, Connecticut, apartment in the late 1940s. Back row (*left to right*): George Bush, Barbara's brothers, James and Scott, Barbara's brother-in-law, Walter G. Rafferty. Front row (*left to right*): Barbara, with son George W. in lap, Pauline Pierce, Marvin Pierce, Barbara's sister, Martha Pierce Rafferty, Barbara's niece Sharon Rafferty. (*Courtesy Scott Pierce*)

George and Barbara before they are married, with George's youngest brother, Bucky. (*Bush Family Album*)

Where Barbara Bush was concerned, it fell somewhere between Washington and Elmendorf Air Force Base in Alaska, at the start of the Far East trip. White House press secretary Marlin Fitzwater told the press corps traveling with the Bushes that there was "no dispute" between Mrs. Bush and the President on banning AK-47s. There would be a statement to that effect upon arrival in Japan, Fitzwater said.

Seven hours later at the Hotel Okura in Tokyo, a spokeswoman for the First Lady, who was admired for her outspokenness by Democrats as well as Republicans in Congress, delivered the word: Barbara Bush would henceforth have no comment on controversial political issues.

3

Straight Shooter

*"I myself do not own a gun. . . . I'm too afraid
I'd shoot the wrong person."*

"*I* hate all thoses things I've said," Barbara Bush lamented as we rode along the San Diego Freeway into Orange County, where she had a campaign appearance that spring day in 1988.

There was no doubt about it; in George Bush's quarter-of-a-century pursuit of the presidency she had said plenty. Not since "Miss Lillian," Jimmy Carter's mother, had there been a woman with White House connections and a habit of speaking out with such flair. And not since Betty Ford had there been the possibility of a First Lady who was as frank as Barbara Bush seemed to be.

She had grown up in a class in which one did

not dwell on oneself—one's name appeared in the public print only at birth, at marriage, and at death. But always talkative and opinionated in private, Barbara had learned to open up in public when George Bush entered politics. She became so skillful at it that by the time she reached 1600 Pennsylvania Avenue, she seemed destined to become one of America's most disarmingly candid First Ladies.

There was no question she tended to be blunt and direct, and that, combined with her self-assurance and assertive manner, was sometimes mistaken for total forthrightness. Like a lot of political wives with sharply tuned antennae about such things, she was capable of withdrawing when pressed about matters that could cause trouble for George. What not everyone always understood was that Barbara revealed as much as she wanted to, but seldom more. She came into the White House with a dexterity at manipulating her image, and she wasn't above playing off her own outspoken style against Nancy Reagan's reluctance and often inability to express herself. Media-smart, a less popular political wife might have seemed calculating.

Not much in life had escaped Barbara's notice, and she had shared her commentary generously. She once estimated she had spoken to a million live faces—and who knows how many sitting in front of television screens. As a candidate's wife, she had no choice. "You go through great self-analysis when you're running for president," she told interviewers more than once. "I feel like I'm on the couch all the time."

So she had talked obligingly about George Bush, their marriage, and their children, doing her best to describe what had made them into the close family they were. She was forthright in interviews, stimulating in conversations, and enormously entertaining in both—when she wanted to be. She could also be sharp-tongued, a talent not insignificant in politics of the 1980s when the press demanded to know not only about candidates' personal finances and health but also whether they had cheated in college, used drugs, harbored homosexual tendencies, or committed adultery.

Barbara Bush faced her share of probing questions about her marriage. The campaign had reopened old wounds with rumors that George Bush had been unfaithful to her. "It wasn't just a brush. It was a large, fat smear and I didn't like it one bit," she told Kathy Lewis of the *Houston Post* in October 1987, shortly after Bush announced his candidacy. That summer, *U.S. News & World Report* and *Newsweek* had reported the gossip, along with angry denials by Bush aides and accusations that people connected with his opponents were waging "a whispering campaign." *Newsweek* reported that oldest son George W. Bush asked his father about the rumors and quoted him as saying, "They're just not true." Barbara told Lewis she had not been pleased that her son's name showed up in connection with the subject "because he opened the door for other people [to ask questions]. But I understood it. If it had been my mother and father, I would have spoken out, too."

(After the election, Lee Atwater admitted to fellow campaign managers that he had engineered the defusing *Newsweek* denial by the younger Bush.)

This day in California she reacted with tight-lipped rage when I questioned her about the gossip that George had had an extramarital affair. "I'm not going to talk about those things anymore. They're boring and I've done it now," Barbara said. But only that morning the whispers had surfaced again, this time on the front page of the *New York Times*. A story by Gerald M. Boyd quoted her as saying she had "hated" the rumors for George's and their family's sakes, but that "George would tell me not to worry, and I didn't worry."

Talking about it to Boyd, she couldn't let well enough alone even then. She recalled another rumor that had made the rounds in Washington early in the Reagan administration: that Bush had been shot during a tryst on Capitol Hill. "I kidded him he ought to call a press conference, strip down, and turn slowly so everybody would know. He was not amused by that," she said.

Now, however, enough was enough, and picking through her box lunch of Chinese egg rolls, she cut off further discussion of the subject. "That's asinine, and you know that," she scolded me. "It's silly to talk about what wasn't and never will be. It's insulting to me." No tantrums and no tears, but no peevish retreat into a pique either. She had made her point and was ready for the next question.

Feisty and articulate, she was what the media regarded as "good copy." Combining—in varying degrees depending upon the situation—intimacy, honesty, and the unexpected with a disarming warmth and natural spontaneity, she said what she thought at times like that—sometimes without too much forethought. "It's part of her problem," was how son George W. put it at the height of the primaries, though more with amusement than alarm.

He knew it was also one of her best attributes. In Washington she stood out in that stifling sorority of political wives schooled in the notion that opinions, like speech, were free but to express them could be ruinously expensive. She had tripped over her candor on occasion, but while her husband's campaign operatives might wince, the public seemed to see her "naturalness" as a plus.

She was well aware of her sometimes brash plain-speaking. "I'm not a good listener," she once said. "I always think ahead and say, 'Well, you're wrong about that.' George thinks when you're asked a question, you're supposed to listen, then answer." About her candor: "The first time I campaigned I probably lost George hundreds of votes. I'm not only outspoken, I'm honest."

Still, it was one thing to be outspoken and quite another to be impudent and caustic, and at times Barbara Bush, the product of finishing schools and genteel upbringing, walked a fine line between the two.

She could deflect with a lash of the tongue. When asked by a reporter how George Bush could justify racing around in his expensive speedboat when there were people starving, she replied, "The American people love boats, everybody has to relax, and"—she took aim at a busy news photographer—"I've got sunblock on but that light of yours is much too close to my face and it's burning me." Sometimes she seemed able to rationalize anything. On a similar question about the needs of the homeless versus the cost of George Bush's inauguration—$30 million, the highest ever—she gazed at me unflinchingly. "You wouldn't raise the money for that purpose [helping the homeless]. These people [the Inaugural Committee] are raising it because they worked for years and years to elect a president. It just couldn't be done. If it could, we would do it. But no, I don't feel badly about it at all. It's [the inauguration] putting a lot of people to work, giving a lot of people jobs. If it were federal money, I'd feel absolutely outraged, but it's not."

She was still haunted by her offhanded 1984 "rhymes with rich" remark about Geraldine Ferraro, made to two reporters aboard Air Force Two on a trip to New York for the Columbus Day parade. The Democrats had been attacking everything from Bush's Ivy League wristwatch band to the family's wealth, and inside, Barbara was fuming. When Terence Hunt of the Associated Press and Ira R. Allen of United Press International pointed out to her that the Bushes weren't exactly paupers, she flung back that at least she and George had never tried to hide it, unlike that "$4 million—I can't say it, but it rhymes with rich."

Neither Hunt nor Allen taped the conversation, but as the Vice President's traveling pool reporters, they had an obligation to file the story. "My position is that anytime you're on a plane and they come back and talk to you, we're all on the record," Hunt said later. In New York, realizing her mistake, Barbara issued a statement saying she regretted the remark. She also apologized to Ferraro, claiming that she really had meant "witch" not "bitch."

"At the time, I was annoyed at her. I thought, 'How does a woman act like that?' I felt that it was a terrible put-down, a terrible class put-down," Ferraro said in 1989. "I was hurt, but I gave her credit for calling as quickly as she did. I told her not to worry about it, that we all say things at times we don't mean. 'Oh, you're such a lady,' she told me. The night of the election, she again got on the phone and was very nice. She's a real person."

It was the most embarrassing situation Barbara had ever gotten herself into and she suffered over it. "I just can't believe I did that to your brother," she told Nancy Ellis soon after. "I've been crying for twenty-four hours and I'll never stop. . . . How could I have done it?" Claiming she had thought her comment was off-the-record, she said publicly, "It hurt me a whole bunch."

Now, in the 1988 primaries and once again aboard Air Force Two, she appeared among pool reporters bristling over Kansas senator Robert J. Dole's campaign rhetoric calling into question just how tough George Bush would be as president. Behind her in the aisle came George, curious about what was going on. Hearing him, she turned on her heels and cut her appearance short. "I better go back to my seat," she said. In a wry gibe at herself she added, "The poet laureate has retired."

After more than four decades, there wasn't much Barbara Bush could have said that would have surprised George Bush. "He knows she's going to speak her mind," said Craig Fuller. "I never saw him say to her, 'Hey, watch what you say.' "

She had long ago established herself within the family as an irreverent wit. "George used to tell me, years ago, 'You've got to tell people that's a joke. People don't know.' My sense of humor is very different," she told Susan Watters of Fairchild News Service in October 1988. "But I only kid people I like. That's a good rule of thumb. If I don't like someone, I'm apt to not kid at all or freeze over slightly. But there are very few people I don't like. I can't think of any."

A good thing, too, because she was an accomplished mimic as well. "She can mimic me," explained Nancy Ellis. "She can mimic her husband, she can mimic the children, she can mimic her friends, or she can mimic the lady that introduced her in such and such a state. She can mimic anybody. In a nice way, I mean. She's not mean." She did a pretty good

Gorbachev and even had been heard to mimic Nancy Reagan on one campaign trip.

She was adept at needling, too, real and otherwise. After Bush won the Iowa caucus in 1980 and claimed to have what he called "the Big Mo"—meaning the momentum to go on to defeat Ronald Reagan—he and Barbara flew on to New Hampshire. *Detroit News* reporter Jerald terHorst, the lone pool reporter on the plane, noticed that she was working on a piece of needlepoint that looked like a seal, maybe even a presidential seal. "That's interesting," terHorst said. "It looks like a seat cover." "It's for George and I'm leaving a needle in it," she replied. "He's got to keep moving."

He didn't make it to the top that time. But here he was, two vice-presidential terms later, making the run again. Riding with reporters on a campaign bus in October, Barbara said she and George had been talking about what would happen after the election. "George Bush said if he loses, on January twentieth he is going to get in a car and drive away from the White House. I said, 'You'll be by yourself because I'm not leaving the White House in a car with a man who's never driven in eight years.' " It wasn't in Barbara to stop teasing, especially after George moved into the Oval Office. "I call him 'Mr. President' sometimes . . . to tease him," she told an interviewer a few days after Bush had assumed that title, then demonstrated: " 'Yes, Mr. President.' "

George wasn't himself so bad at needling. After

one of her characteristic jabs at the way he was handling something, he might sound off: If he had needed her opinion, he would have made her a member of his staff. He rolled with her punches, but she also rolled with his. One of the things that had attracted her to him was his own wit, something he often resorted to when tensions were high; with a reputation as thin-skinned, Bush's saving grace was that he could usually laugh at himself in private.

Their families had lived less than ten miles apart as they were growing up, and their fathers almost certainly had a nodding acquaintance on the golf course long before their offspring met at a dance, but George and Barbara didn't take their upper-crust togetherness too seriously. "The streak that separates Barbara and George from their formal and traditional family backgrounds," said Vic Gold, coauthor of Bush's autobiography *Looking Forward*, "was their irreverence towards who they are at any given time."

Bickering wasn't any more a part of the Bush style than serious goading was. At Kennebunkport in August 1988, as the two of them sat on the stone wall outside their Walker's Point house, Barbara told me that "George is not a good quarreler—he doesn't like to quarrel, he likes to discuss."

"So does she," he said.

"Well, I used to like to quarrel," she reminded him in joking reference to her adjustment to his style.

For George Bush, her tongue had seemed sharp at times and took some getting used to. "I remember

George said to me once when we were first married, 'You know, you ridiculed me in public, Bar, and I wish you wouldn't do that.' Well, it was just a dumb thing, but he was dead right, and I never did it again."

As the wife of a politician she was a paradox to many. While loyal to traditional Republican dogma, she seemed to be sometimes independent on controversial issues, and—compared to her husband—almost liberal. During the 1980 campaign, for instance, she was on the other side of the fence, supporting gun control, voicing her apparently long-standing views in an interview with *Washington Star* reporter Judy Bachrach.

"You know George has always been against gun control. Well, I have always been for gun control," she said. "For thirty-five years I have been for gun control. Now this should give you two deep insights on the situation. The first insight is what great influence I have on George Bush. And the second is how George feels about gun control. . . . It's just a thing with me, how I feel about gun control. I just don't feel it's any big deal to register a gun."

But as George Bush's political star brightened, Barbara toned down her own views, at least when they conflicted with her husband's. In 1980 she told Bachrach, "I support the Equal Rights Amendment, but that is not a major item with me." By 1989, she told Iris Krasnow of United Press International that "George voted for ERA. That went through the states. That had its shot. Why knock yourself out on something that's had a chance? Why not just work for equal rights for all Americans, instead of just banging your head?"

On abortion, when she reluctantly talked about it, she sometimes left the impression that she disagreed with George's evolving public stand against it simply because she declined to commit herself publicly. "I have never told anybody about my feelings about abortion," she told the *New York Times*' Gamarekian. In 1989, during a session with reporters at the White House, she went so far as to say she was "grateful" that a February U.S. Supreme Court decision permitted Martin Klein of Long Island to authorize an abortion for his comatose wife in hopes it would lead to her recovery. She refused, however, to criticize antiabortion activists who had tried to block the procedure. "I'm not going to get into that." But she did say, "I'm very grateful that it worked out as it did. I agree with my husband on that. The life of the mother was at risk."

Klein said later he interpreted Barbara's remark as "supportive of the outcome. But I think what she was attempting to say was she didn't want to get into a debate on abortion, other than that she was happy the decision worked out in our particular favor." Antiabortion activist John Short, who attempted to block the abortion by challenging Klein's guardianship, called Barbara "misinformed at the time." He took a train to Washington from Farmingdale, New York, to see her, but when he was unsuccessful left her a letter. "Mrs. Bush thanks you for writing and appreciates the benefit of your thoughts," went the official reply to Short's letter.

In the White House, as she had during the campaign, Barbara was attempting to walk a fine line. "I'm slightly more careful about what I say," she had told *Time* magazine just before the inauguration. "Slightly."

To some in the media, there had been signs that she was biting her tongue as early as fall 1987. Bush, who had just formally announced his candidacy, decided to appear on NBC's *Meet the Press*. On the panel was *Washington Post* political columnist David Broder, whose intention was to explore questions about how in touch Bush was with the man on the street. Did Bush know how many Americans had no health insurance or what percentage of the unemployed were not covered by unemployment compensation? Broder asked.

"I don't know the answer to it, no," Bush said.

At the Bushes' annual Christmas party a few days later, the Vice President was affable as usual when Broder went through the receiving line. Barbara was also agreeable but typically, let Broder know that she was well aware of what he had been up to. She instantly calibrated the way she wanted to say it.

"You son of a gun, those questions you asked!" she told him.

"Barbara," Broder replied, laughing, "you can talk more plainly than that."

"Not me," she countered. "We're running for president."

Her political instincts were sharp and she was skilled at artful dodging. But she could also blurt out things seemingly without thinking. Two weeks to the day after Bush took the oath of office, she made an off-the-cuff remark that set in motion forces that would have far-reaching consequences before another month had passed. The AP's Hunt had just read something about former presidential press secretary Jim Brady, who had been wounded in the 1981 assassination attempt on Ronald Reagan, and remembered that Barbara was a friend of Brady's. He asked Barbara how she felt about guns.

"She said something about the gun scare—I was asking her about handguns—but said she didn't want to get into a big discussion about guns, that it was a political issue," Hunt remembered. Urging Hunt to talk to her husband about his position on handguns, she said, "I myself do not own a gun. I choose not to get into that. I am afraid of them. I'm too afraid I'd shoot the wrong person." Hunt said she volunteered a story about the time she went hunting with Bush. "He told me to follow the bird, and I followed the bird and his head came right through that little circle [the rifle scope]. I put down the gun and said, 'That's it. I'm not going to do that again.' "

Hunt asked what she thought about those military-style assault weapons such as the one Patrick Edward Purdy used to kill five children at a Stockton, California, schoolyard in mid-January 1989. "She said those were illegal, and I said, 'No, I don't think they are. The AK-47s aren't illegal. Do you think they should be?' She said, 'Absolutely.' There was no hesitation, she was very firm about that."

Within a week, standing behind his campaign promise to oppose additional federal gun control laws, George Bush told reporters that he was "not about to say semiautomatic hunting rifles ought to be banned. Absolutely not." On February 16, in an Oval Office session with reporters, he reiterated that he did not support legislation that would ban the import of the AK–47s because he believed that it was up to the states, which had "a lot of laws on these things," to crack down on criminals. It was his position and he wasn't going to change it, he said.

On Capitol Hill, Barbara Bush's offhanded remark assumed new importance, becoming fodder for advocates of gun control legislation. "What Bush ought to do is listen to Barbara," said Senator Paul Simon, the Illinois Democrat who had chaired Senate hearings on legislation to impose restrictions on the weapons.

Around the country, antigun groups were finding unexpected new support for banning assault rifles from police leaders. Among the most eloquent was Los Angeles Police Chief Daryl F. Gates, who had been a campaign adviser to Bush on drugs and crime. "I do not want any more officers to be spray-gunned to death by street punks armed with high-tech killing machines," he told a Senate hearing. Politicians previously considered soft on the issue joined the movement. But the President was also being pressured by powerful opposing forces. Representatives of the National Rifle Association, who met at the White House with high-ranking Bush advisers, attempted to shift the focus to Purdy, running advertisements proclaiming that seven times "the system" had set him free. The ads pointed out that Purdy's arrest record lacked the felony convictions on sex, weapons, drugs, and robbery charges, which would have barred him from buying an AK-47 under existing laws.

Meanwhile, Barbara, who had become the heroine of the antigun groups, was undergoing some pressures from within her own family. "I told her that she may be expressing her opinion," said son Jeb, "but that it's a very complicated issue, as people are starting to figure out now. And that the emotional side of it might be, 'Hell, let's just ban [the AK-47],' but that there are constitutional questions and there are regional differences." Jeb, who unlike his father never took up hunting, acknowledged that her impromptu remark probably enhanced her popularity. "But I know there are lots of folks out there using this issue to try to accomplish a larger goal, which is abolition of gun ownership in general or of a whole class of weapons. And that's not what my mom was talking about. And she may have helped encourage that," he said. "Now that she's the First Lady, anything she says is going to be thrown out there. And no matter what context it's said in, it's going to be interpreted verbatim the way it comes out. So it's a pretty powerful position."

George's sister, Nancy Ellis, had a different reaction. She thought what Barbara said was "great" and that "it might have stirred [George] on." By helping bring things to the attention of her brother, she saw promise of an Eleanor Roosevelt in Barbara. "It's all just a political decision, I think," she said. "I mean, I can't believe my brother isn't for limiting those. He never wants to shoot anything except a quail. For a Navy pilot going around bombing things, he never ever wanted to fly again. There's none of that top-gun, take-out-of-the-sky attitude."

By late February, Barbara took steps to remove herself from the eye of the storm by buttoning her lip on gun control, and while she was at it, every other issue of a controversial nature. She made her first public stab at withdrawing during an NBC News interview with Jim Miklaszewski in which she said her position was no different from her husband's on gun control. Anna Perez made it official in Tokyo.

"She's not the one who makes policy. She's not the one who lobbies Congress. She's not the president of the United States. To that extent, her opinions are not the ones that should be the focus," Perez told reporters gathered around her in the White House press center at the Acura Hotel.

"No one is muzzling her?" a reporter asked.

"Not that I know of," Perez replied.

"What if we think her opinions are important?" asked United Press International correspondent Helen Thomas.

"Shame on you," replied Perez.

"Shame on me for saying the First Lady has a right to an opinion?" Thomas asked, her voice brittle with irony.

"It doesn't mean she doesn't have a right to an opinion," countered Perez. "She has a right to express one or not."

Asked later if the conversation with Jeb had contributed to the statement, Barbara said, "No, I don't think so. Jebby and I talked. I didn't understand what's legal and what's illegal. He tried to explain to me [that] it's more complicated than I know. You see, I don't want to diffuse. The reason I don't talk about the gun control or other issues is because I have some things I really want to get done and in order to get them done, I can't get off on those very controversial things I can't make a difference about anyway. I'm not an elected official."

But by early March, George, who *was* the elected official, gave signs of backing off from his earlier position. Indicating that he might be open to restrictions on the AK-47s, Bush announced he had asked the administration's drug czar, William J. Bennett, to explore ways to restrict the guns and still "do what's right by the legitimate sportsman." By mid-March, as drug-related murders reached alarming proportions on Washington streets, Bush agreed to a temporary ban on the importation of the rifle. "Thank God for Barbara Bush," said Chief Gates on national television. On May 15, Bush announced the ban would be permanent and that he would propose legislation to ban not only the import but also the manufacture and sale of semiautomatic weapon magazines capable of firing more than fifteen rounds.

Like it or not, Barbara was getting a big share of the credit. But if she could have done it over, Barbara would surely have done it differently—she would have disagreed in private, as was her habit, according to what she told that group of reporters at the Vice President's House. Would she be candid with him? "Oh, very candid. That's why we do so well. I tell him what I think, he tells me what he thinks. Then we are united."

For his part, George too would have dealt with troublesome issues privately. If he had a complaint, he might tell her he wished she hadn't said or done a certain thing, but he would also urge her not to worry about it. He had encouraged independence in his children as they were growing up, and he admired her independent nature. He sounded almost avuncular about it in a Barbara Walters interview aired on ABC News' *20/20* on inauguration night. "I'm going to approach my job as Barbara is approaching hers," he said. "Call them the way you see them, as that umpire said."

Calling them the way she saw them came naturally to Barbara Pierce Bush, who as a child, had been encouraged to say what she thought. Competition for attention was brisk within the Pierce family, and those who triumphed needed a keen sense of humor, couldn't take themselves too seriously, and had to tell a story more amusingly than anybody else. On all those counts, Barbara took after her father.

4

Rye Times

"I was a very happy fat child who spent all my life with my mother saying 'Eat up, Martha' to my older sister and 'Not you, Barbara.' "

*H*istory may never know how much she weighed when she was born, since it was not recorded on the birth certificate. But for Barbara Pierce—born June 8, 1925 in New York City—weight would become a fixation while she was growing up. Even in her sixties, she was not above exaggerating her birth weight—"probably one hundred," she jokingly told me when asked about it in an interview at the White House in 1989. She was the third of Marvin and Pauline Robinson Pierce's four children, timing she later called "clearly the best—all the pressure's off—particularly if you have one of

each sex above you because it means everything's
been seen through."

The family had moved to Rye, New York,
shortly before she was born, but her mother's obste-
trician practiced one month a year at Booth Memorial, a maternity hospital on Manhattan's Lower East
Side operated by the Salvation Army primarily—but
not exclusively—for unwed mothers. So when labor
pains began, Marvin Pierce bundled his twenty-nine-
year-old wife into the family car for the hour-long
drive into Manhattan.

Marvin, by then thirty-one and assistant to the
publisher of the McCall Corporation, had wanted to
name his second daughter Helen—he had had three
good friends named Helen—but his wife had preferred Catherine. "He stood firm and she stood firm,"
Barbara said, "so they called me Barbara." And they
left it at that, with no middle name.

For five years she was the baby of the family.
Then a fourth child, a son, was born. By the time he
was two, doctors informed the Pierces that he had a
cyst—"a bad place," as Barbara, her sister, Martha,
and brother James were told—in the bone marrow
of his shoulder. For the next seven years, Scott Pierce
was in and out of New York City hospitals undergoing bone scrapings and grafts, and his mother went
daily to be with him. Desperate about her son, Pauline
suffered the heavy emotional toll of not knowing if
the boy would ever get well. Though Marvin provided the stability his family needed, he agonized quietly over Scott's condition. Once, driving home from

New York where X rays had been taken to determine whether anything further could be done for the child, Marvin was pulled over to the side of the road for speeding. By then nine years old but unaware that he was in jeopardy, Scott watched his father break into tears as he told the policeman that he had just taken his son in to see if he was going to lose his arm.

Though years later Barbara would empathize with her mother, as a child she had not understood the strain her brother's illness had placed on Pauline. "My mother, I'm sure, was tired and irritable and I didn't understand it at the time. But I guess I felt neglected, that she didn't spend as much time on me. She had this enormous responsibility, which I was never sympathetic about. Now as a mother and grandmother, I realize what she was going through."

Deprived of the maternal attention she once had, Barbara turned to her father, a man of steady perspective whose enjoyment of sports fostered her own lifelong love of them. "He was every letter-man you can think of. . . . He was a great athlete." Pauline was another matter. "My mother wasn't interested. If your mother isn't interested in something she's not going to get the girls interested. I think you need a competitive mother," explained Barbara, who called Pauline "a very good mother" but said, "I did not have a great relationship with her."

Pauline, born in 1896 in Marysville, Ohio, was one of four children of James and Lulu Robinson, her father being a member of the Buckeye State's first supreme court. Pauline attended Oxford College in

Oxford, Ohio, where as the campus beauty she met Marvin Pierce, the campus hero at nearby Miami University.

Marvin, one of two children, was born in 1893 in Sharpsville, Pennsylvania, into the wealthy Pierce clan, who owned an iron foundry. Among their early relatives was America's fourteenth president, Franklin Pierce. Marvin Pierce's children never played up that relationship, which Barbara said was "more like a great-great-great-uncle." As a child, the only thing she remembered about him "was reading that he was one of our weakest presidents. I was humiliated."

The crash of the iron market in 1893 brought hard times for the Pierces, from which Barbara's grandfather Scott Pierce never recovered. Marvin delayed going to college for two years, working as a surveyor and as a teaching assistant in botany to help support the family. Entering Miami University in 1912, he became Phi Beta Kappa, a pitcher on the baseball team, a trophy-winning tennis player, and captain of the football team.

After graduating summa cum laude, Marvin went on to MIT and Harvard College, earning degrees in civil and architectural engineering. He joined the U.S. Army Corps of Engineers and went overseas, but missed the fighting. After working as an engineer for a time, he joined the McCall Publishing Company in 1921. Named a vice president of the corporation in 1926, by 1934 he was a director, and was elected company president in 1946.

In New York, Marvin and Pauline, who married in 1918, started out in a walk-up coldwater flat. It wasn't unusual for the two of them to arrive before sunrise at a public golf course, where Marvin put his marked ball in a trough to establish his turn, then teed off when the sun came up. Pauline was "the least athletic woman in the world, so I'm sure her idea of nothing was to go out [golfing]," Barbara said, "but she did it because she loved him very much." Eventually, she was also pregnant, so she exercised by walking the course with Marvin.

Pauline was a woman of what her children called "enthusiasms." She was a fervid gardener who became an expert on the pollination of lillies. She also grew flats of barley in the basement, where she raised worms to aerate her garden soil. During World War II, she tilled Victory Gardens in several Rye locations, collected huge balls of tinfoil for recycling, and though an out-of-practice violinist, kept one war-bond rally audience captive with her playing.

She was a soft touch for nature's wounded, hospitalizing injured squirrels in the bathtub and mending the broken wings of birds. But worried that starlings were driving away the desirable birds, she paid her sons twenty-five cents for every starling they shot with a BB gun. Since meat was being rationed, once she baked an elaborate starling pie and presented it at the dinner table to her startled family. "She dipped in and pulled out one the size of a golf ball, with the legs off, and everybody else passed," remembered

Scott. "She got kind of upset about that." Luckily, the cook, suspecting the pie might not go over, came along behind with a meatless vegetable stew.

She was "absolutely ravishing," in Barbara's memory. "When you look at all the [Ohio] pictures —George has spoken there and I've spoken there and gone out with my dad—and you see all these class pictures, and she's the pretty one. She's always the pretty one in the pictures."

She had an eye for the beauty of gracious surroundings, too. She did the finest needlepoint Barbara ever saw and was an avid collector of antique china, crystal, and furniture. Growing up in those surroundings was hazardous for four rambunctious children. "Every time you turned around, you knocked a piece of Chinese export off the table," Barbara told an interviewer years later. Pauline never said a word, but she didn't have to; her face reflected the pain of her loss. "She was not perfect, but I always think the world was more beautiful because my mother was there," said Barbara. "She taught us all a lot of good lessons."

Ironically, some of what Barbara learned was to approach life differently from Pauline. Though she believed her mother to be happy enough, she also recognized that Pauline was one of those people who enjoyed thinking that things were going to be better later. "She always thought the grass was going to be greener sometime, some other place. . . . I don't believe that. I believe life is right now. And I think my mother taught me that."

Pauline Pierce had another problem: keeping up with the Joneses, of whom there were many in the quiet Westchester County town of 8,000 on Long Island Sound. At the turn of the century, Rye had been a summer community for New Yorkers. By the time the Pierces settled in, traces of that era remained, but Rye was gradually being transformed into a bedroom community for Manhattan.

The Pierces paid $14,500 for the three-story, five-bedroom brick house with garage on Onondaga Street, in an area known as Indian Village. Set among big trees on a quarter-acre lot, the house was surrounded by gardens, featuring an artificial pond. The house seemed gigantic at the time, though after a "Welcome Home Barbara Bush Day" years later Barbara decided it had shrunk and marveled that the six Pierces and their live-in help—a three-member Filipino family at one time—had managed to fit in.

It was a Social Register community of affluent families whose fathers played golf all weekend and mothers beautified the town all week—or, at least, when they weren't working as volunteers for the hospital service league, attending meetings of the Great Books Club, or playing bridge. Pauline, who would eventually become conservation chairman of the Garden Clubs of America, persuaded Rye's town fathers to bar parking on the main street so it could be turned into a pedestrian thoroughfare and adorned with hanging baskets. "When you talk about a joiner," said Barbara Bush, "you're talking about my mother."

It was a lifestyle that also took money—of which

Pauline Pierce never had quite enough. "If you gave her ten dollars, she'd spend twenty dollars," Barbara remembered. In status-conscious Rye, the financial strain caused by young Scott's illness coupled with the fact that Pauline was not one who budgeted very well—"to put it mildly"—meant that she was always "one step behind," at least in paying her bills. But her children never wanted for anything. "No, of course not," said Barbara. "She charged it!" In the drawer next to her mother's bed were always unpaid bills of such numbers that when Barbara wanted to buy a coat, for instance, Pauline would caution, "Now, don't go to Best when you go buy that coat, go over to Lord and Taylor's because I owe Best."

Shortly before Barbara wed George Bush, her father took her to lunch in New York City to talk to her about marriage. The biggest problem, he told her, was that people couldn't handle money. She listened quietly to his lecture on the importance of living within a budget, then finally asked how in the world he, of all people, could say such a thing, given his wife's spendthrift ways. Pauline Pierce was different, Barbara's father admitted, explaining how he handled this woman he adored. "What I do is, I give her half what I can afford to give her. And then," he said, "at Christmas and at our anniversary I give her the other half. And she thinks I'm a hero all the time."

Nobody knew how undisciplined she had been with her money until after her death in 1949. According to Barbara, vendors from around the country turned up to inform Marvin Pierce that his wife had made deposits on antique furniture they were holding for her. Barbara never doubted that it was true—"I mean, she bought on the installment plan all over America. And nobody dared say, 'Well, Mrs. Pierce never would have done that' because the truth was, she would have."

As an adult, Barbara recalled her childhood as one surrounded by "luxury." But while the Republican Pierces were far removed from the hardships of the Great Depression elsewhere in America, they were not as well off as many of their friends in Rye. Barbara's brother Scott said he had been shocked to learn from McCall's that his father, who died in 1969 and only owned one hundred shares of the firm's stock, had a loan outstanding of $100,000.

But none of that was evident when Barbara was growing up. She was tall for her age, a somewhat pudgy girl for whom life began and ended in her Indian Village neighborhood. Years later, describing it in interviews, she found it difficult to imagine growing up in a better place. Her first and last trip away to summer camp came when she was twelve, weighed 148 pounds, and by her own description "looked like Porky Pig and probably should have gone to a diet camp." She had worried the entire time that back in Rye everybody was having fun while she was isolated. When an illness swept through the camp forcing it to close, she returned home, liberated.

There Barbara's life was an endless round of riding bicycles, cutting out paper dolls, and playing "imagination" games: Lucille Schoolfield liked to be

Albert Payson Terhune, a children's writer who specialized in dog stories. Barbara, June Biedler, Kate Siedel, and Posy Morgan always had to be the dogs. Lucille taught them about Santa Claus and what boys and girls did together, and standing on the sidewalk in front of the house, she read love poems by Rupert Brooke aloud to them. There was tamer literature, too. "We all loved Louisa May Alcott's *Little Women* and played the parts in our make-believe games," Barbara said.

Of course, there were magazines, too, which in those days featured serial stories. "I really waited monthly for the next installment of those things. And when I got to boarding school, they told me that was trash reading. And I told my dad, 'You can't send me those magazines anymore, it's trash reading.' He said, 'Look, you tell them that trash is sending you to school.' "

Neighbors were like extended families whose children were wandering tribes of rope-jumpers and tree-climbers. They grew up in groups—in each other's backyards and taking tennis and swimming lessons at the Manursing Island Club on Long Island Sound. On weekends and in summer, they were dropped off at nine A.M. and picked up at six P.M., as punctual as the arrival of the 5:23 New Haven and Hartford commuter train that brought their fathers home from Manhattan. Friendships were forever, interrupted but never broken by departures for boarding school.

Friday night was Miss Covington's Dancing

School, which taught Barbara not only to waltz but also to deal with the realities of life, among them a shortage of boys. "My mother would say, 'You must not be the boy every time.' " For Barbara, though, standing on the sidelines as a dwindling number of boys first bowed, then asked a girl to dance, there was no other practical solution. "I didn't want to be left. Not me. I was five feet eight at the age of twelve." And while she said her height did not bother her even then, "it certainly bothered the boys."

She was a tomboy at heart, eventually demanding joint tenancy in a tree house Marvin Pierce had built in the front yard for the boys. Dogs were the love of her life long before boys. First there were Scotties, then cairn terriers—Barbara had her own, named Sandy—and periodically Pauline's little female would have puppies. When that happened, the senior Pierces' bathroom, one of two on the second floor, became a maternity ward, and Barbara's father exploded. "I can remember my father saying, 'Damn!'—I mean, we're talking small bathroom— 'Damn! When do I get my bathroom back? Got up in the middle of the night and then stepped on a puppy!' "

Boys had their turn in her life about the time coed Saturday bike rides preempted tree houses, *Little Women*, and paper dolls. None of her crushes were memorable with the exception of one beau who, surviving the separation of winters, would be welcomed back at Manursing Island each summer to an enduring if only hand-holding romance with Barbara.

She was a popular, fun-loving, and outgoing youngster who idolized her sister, Martha, was "scared to death—he was so naughty" of her brother James, and adored her brother Scott, for whom she was kind of "a second mother." Weekday mornings she and Scott usually walked with their father as far as the train station, then took a bus on to school.

Martha, five years older than Barbara, remembered her sister as always at war with James. Martha went off to a southern boarding school a tall, thin, gawky ugly duckling and returned a beauty with brains to match. She became a Smith College legend before she ever graduated, discovered by *Vogue* magazine and immortalized on its cover as its "College Girl of the Year."

James, three years Barbara's senior, was a devilishly mischievous boy who suffered his mother's stern discipline more than the others. "The way to punish us was to have us go out and stand by the door and pose," Barbara remembered. "You know, you took a stand for half an hour." Barbara's fear of James was not without justification. Once, he accidentally shot her in the leg with a BB gun but warned that if she told their mother, he would "kill" her. Barbara could be a merciless tease who could hardly wait to expose James's misdeeds, but that time she thought better of it. "For a week I wore long, high woolen socks and feared death," she revealed years later in a speech at American University.

Barbara remembered Scott as uncomplaining and unspoiled, despite all the attention their mother gave him. He was an enthusiastic child, interested in everything: the nuthatches his mother rescued and deputized him to feed; the trouble his brother, James, got into; his sisters' beaus; the story about the six-fingered great-uncle who used to visit Grandfather Pierce. Barbara told me she'd always heard that story but never saw any six-fingered relatives and wondered if it was a myth.

Though the Pierces were Protestants, Friday was fish night because Pauline said fish was good for everybody. Barbara said it also meant that the children's Roman Catholic friends, usually "starved" by their other friends' Protestant mothers on Fridays, had something to eat if they came to the Pierces'. Only Scott was served meat. "Scottie Pierce did not like fish," Barbara remembered, laughing. "And I can remember the little master would get the lamb chop as we'd all be eating fish."

The family's time together at the dinner table was as notable for its emphasis on eating habits as it was for moments of togetherness it provided, a magazine theme the McCall Corporation would subsequently adopt under her father's presidency to point up "every facet of family living—the aspirations, excitements, and activities of a life fully shared."

"That's the way I think of my childhood, at the table," she told United Press International during the 1988 campaign. "We had wonderful food at our house. We always had real cream on our cereal and mashed potatoes made from the real McCoy." But she remembered something else about those meals, too. "I was a very happy fat child who spent all my life with my mother saying 'Eat up, Martha' to my older sister and 'Not you, Barbara.' "

"Actually, I was much closer to my father and probably the child least close to my mother," she said. Marvin Pierce had a contagious sense of humor and was a great tease whose children took after him in that regard. Pauline, in contrast, had "no sense of humor," according to Barbara, and more often than not her "enthusiasms" were the center of their jokes. Marvin was Barbara's hero, her favorite. And maybe the feeling was mutual; he always took her side—"I think because Mother never took my side," Barbara once said. Marvin believed there were only three things parents could give their children: "A fine education, a good example, and all the love in the world."

Barbara's formal education began in 1931 at Rye's public Milton School. Her mother, leading her by the hand, took her to meet the teacher. Barbara remembered that Pauline "disappeared with no goodbyes. I felt abandoned. But I truly loved school so much I forgave her by the time I got home." She stayed at Milton through the sixth grade, then entered the private Rye Country Day School. Her junior year she left Rye to attend a small, exclusive preparatory school in Charleston, South Carolina, where the emphasis was on classical education with attention to the hallmarks of good breeding. Pauline had chosen Ashley Hall for both daughters in the belief they should be exposed to "different" areas of the country. Certainly, it had transformed Martha into a stunning young woman, and there was no reason to think that a similar metamorphosis might not be possible in Barbara.

Susan Estey Edgerly, who became a roommate of Barbara's, remembered that they all wore a purple and white ribbon when they arrived at Grand Central Station in New York City that September day in 1941 for the overnight train trip to Charleston. Barbara remembered "a lot of fat, squatty girls" bound for Ashley Hall. She was desolate, an emotional state that continued all the way to the school. "I distinctly remember walking up the long flight of stairs to the third floor. I felt miserable for about four minutes," she told the *Charleston News & Courier* years later, "until I got to know some other girls."

Of the 150 students, about half were boarders whose lives were dictated by a set of rules that forbade them to wear makeup, leave campus without hats, gloves, and stockings, or date the same boy two weekends in a row. Headmistress Mary Vardrine McBee, who had founded the school thirty years earlier, was adamant that no love affairs be allowed to develop at Ashley Hall. Barbara, who had no steady beaus but occasionally saw a friend of Martha's, a cadet from The Citadel, sometimes played Cupid for Cordelia Lambert Stites, another roommate, by trading off boyfriends for a parlor date. Dating in full view of a dozen or so other couples wasn't anybody's idea of romance, but it was better than nothing, so girls signed up in advance for two seats in the parlor between two and four o'clock on Sunday afternoons.

Since singing was not one of her strong points, Barbara was asked to be the Speaking Angel in the drama club's 1941 Christmas pageant. It was one of several dramatic roles she would take on in her junior and senior years for which critical acclaim was not recorded, though schoolmates gave her high marks for at least knowing her lines. She played Beatrice in Shakespeare's *Much Ado About Nothing* and Viola in *Twelfth Night*. She was school record-holder at speed-knitting, at swimming underwater (two and a half times across the pool), and at eating the most hot, buttered biscuits in one meal without being caught.

World War II started in December of her junior year. Miss McBee announced the chilling news of the bombing of Pearl Harbor during the drama club's after-church rehearsal of the annual Christmas pageant. Frantically, girls called home to hear reassurances that their families were safe. Everybody felt dangerously close to the war.

A few days later, back home in Rye for the holidays, sixteen-year-old Barbara Pierce would meet the boy who would soon bring the war even closer.

5

Love at First Sight

"I married the first man I ever kissed. When I tell this to my children, they just about throw up."

S/*he* was a tall, slender girl with naturally wavy reddish-brown hair, wearing a red and green, off-the-shoulder dress, and he watched her move around the dance floor while the orchestra was playing some Glenn Miller tune. What struck him about her was her vitality, her large, laughing eyes, and the fun she was having. He wasn't much of a dancer, and unlike friends sharing the sidelines with him that night at the Round Hill Country Club in Greenwich, Connecticut, he was reticent about cutting in. But when he saw that the girl was dancing with Jack Wozencraft, a tennis-club mate who was home from Deerfield Academy for the holidays,

Poppy Bush decided to find out who she was. When the dance was finished, Poppy went over. Did he want to meet her? asked Wozencraft, who lived in Rye and had grown up with Barbara Pierce. "I told him that was the general idea," Bush later wrote in his autobiography, *Looking Forward.*

Introductions over, Poppy—as George's uncles had nicknamed him after their father and his namesake, George Herbert Walker—asked Barbara to dance. Everybody wore tuxedos and long dresses, but formality never went so far as to include dance cards, so she readily accepted, but right about then the orchestra struck up a waltz. Since Poppy didn't waltz, they decided to sit it out, which they did for several more dances even though Barbara had a beau at the time.

Both had come with their own groups that night, Poppy with the one from Greenwich and Barbara with the one from Rye. Though they had grown up just a few miles apart and their parents often belonged to the same clubs, the two teenage sets seldom mixed socially except at special parties arranged by the clubs. Sometimes, they went to dinner at somebody's home before they arrived at the dance. Once the music started, there was an "occasional exuberance" of jitterbugging but seldom at the expense of more traditional dancing, remembered Wozencraft, himself an alumnus of Miss Covington. Thirst was quenched by unspiked punch, conduct watched by chaperones, and outside, the family chauffeurs waited to take everybody home.

Whatever it was Barbara and George talked about

that night—she said later it was not the Navy, which he had made up his mind by then to join—it made a lasting impression on both. "I could hardly breathe when he was in the room," was how she described the effect he had had on her. Nancy Ellis never got over thinking how prescient her brother had been at the age of seventeen to recognize in a girl so young the qualities he admired and would later depend upon so much. "I think he saw a person sure enough of herself to reach out to others and not be worried about herself all the time. And they're much the same qualities that my mother had."

Barbara, too, saw something she liked. "He was just a very attractive young man. I went home and told my mother," she said. "Now here's something my mother did that really burned me up. I slept in the next morning, and when I woke up, my mother said, 'Well, I just asked Maggie, she knows them well.' I said, 'You asked about someone I met last night?' Maggie was her greatest, best friend. She said, 'Oh, she knows them well.' That took a little of the glow off."

That night George came to the Apawamis Club exchange dance in Rye. "He literally cut in on me and asked if he and I could have a date. And my brother cut in on him, which was unforgivable in my eyes since he hated me—James—and he did it because he was trying to get a basketball team to play another team in Rye and he said, 'Are you Poppy Bush?' He said yes. James said, 'Well, you go and wait in the corner and I'll be right over.'"

But not all was lost. George asked if he could drive Barbara home after the game, which was to be played a few nights later. The first that Barbara's younger brother Scott realized there was something potentially romantic going on was when Barbara, who'd shown no interest in basketball in her sixteen years, announced that she thought everybody ought to go see a game at the YMCA. They did. "My whole family came down and looked at him—everybody," Barbara remembered. Meanwhile, George, a nice-looking, skinny kid, though not much of a basketball player, worried that Barbara and he might not have much to say to each other. He begged his parents to let him borrow the family's big car, the one with the radio. As it turned out, he need not have bothered. Years later he would tease that she started talking that night and hadn't stopped since.

After the Christmas holidays, Barbara returned to Ashley Hall, which, like everyplace else in Charleston, was girding up for the war. The dining hall was sandbagged as a bomb shelter, air-raid drills replaced fire drills, and when the siren went off, as it did from time to time, no one could be sure whether it was just another drill or the enemy was approaching. Once in 1942, fear swept the campus at a rumor that a German submarine had been sighted off the South Carolina coast; twenty years later the Navy verified that the Coast Guard had sunk a sub off Cape Lookout on May 9, 1942.

It was an emotional time as brothers and boy-friends were going off to battle and the girls they left behind thought about being in love. George Bush was still a student, back at Andover, but Barbara Pierce talked so much about the boy she had met during the holidays that it didn't take long for her roommates to realize that Poppy Bush was more than just a crush.

She was a conscientious student, usually doing her homework cross-legged on her bed. When she wasn't studying, she sat there knitting argyle socks for Poppy, or writing him letters. The long white envelopes postmarked Andover moved in and out of her mailbox almost daily. She shared portions of his letters with her close friends, reading them aloud because that's what all the girls did. "None of the mushy stuff, just the very newsy parts," Cordelia Lambert Stites said years later. "But we never allowed the other person to actually have the letter in her hands." No one will know exactly what George's letters said because Barbara didn't save them, "darn it."

Andover, Massachusetts, and Charleston, South Carolina, were a thousand miles apart, and Barbara and George saw each other only once that spring, when their breaks overlapped by a day. At the end of the year George took her to his senior prom. George wrote about his graduation in his autobiography. Secretary of War Henry Stimson delivered the commencement address, predicting a long war and advising his audience that while America needed fighting men, young men such as those seated before him could serve their country better by going on with their education. But George had made his decision months before; he was going to enlist in the Navy as soon as he was eighteen. When his father, Prescott Bush, asked if Stimson had said anything to change his mind, George said, "No, sir. I'm going in." His birthday was June 12—he was 361 days older than Barbara—and the day he turned eighteen he was in Boston signing up as a seaman second class. He was soon in preflight training in Chapel Hill, North Carolina.

In the year that followed, Barbara, by then a senior at Ashley Hall, visited once. George, looking no more than a child himself—when he did get his wings he was the youngest pilot in the Navy—was waiting for her at the station. Earlier, he had asked Pauline Pierce for a picture of Barbara, and she'd sent a young-looking one of Barbara with her dog, Sandy. For this visit, George asked Barbara to fib a little about her age. "Tell people that you're eighteen—I've told everybody you're eighteen," he urged her. "Well, of course," she said years later, "not a living human asked me how old I was."

A year later, in June 1943, Barbara and her twenty-nine Ashley Hall classmates heard the chaplain from the Charleston Navy yard deliver their commencement address. Though there were many opportunities for the youth of that day, they were not necessarily automatic ones, Lieutenant Commander Roy E. LeMoine told his young audience. They had to be protected. "Things without which people will be unable to build a good world are education, religion, and the consciousness that they cannot live a selfish and secure life," the local newspaper

reported him as saying. Forty-one years later, at another Ashley Hall commencement where she was this
time the speaker, the former Barbara Pierce confessed
that she remembered nothing about LeMoine's commencement address—and had even forgotten his
name. There was a similar ring to their messages,
however. "Much has been given you and therefore,
much is expected of you," counseled the school's
most famous alumna.

That summer, George invited Barbara up to
Maine to be with him and his family before he went
on to advanced flight training. She went for seventeen
days and was a great hit with Dorothy Bush, who, the
story has it, later told Pauline Pierce that Barbara
could make the most wonderful peanut butter sandwiches. "He had these two baby brothers, eight and
five, and the mother and father went out one night,
and she said, 'Would you mind making dinner?' I
mean to tell you, she had everything out to make
sandwiches for the boys—it may well have been peanut butter. Anyway, we had sandwiches, fruit, ice
cream or something. My mother ran into Mrs. Bush
later, and Mrs. Bush looked my mother straight in the
face and said, 'You have the most wonderful daughter. Do you know that that blessed child made sandwiches for everybody and fed our house one night
when she was our guest?' " It showed two things,
Barbara liked to point out in later years: that Dorothy
Bush always found something good to say about
someone, and that there may not have been much else
good worth saying about Barbara at that point.

In Maine, George and Barbara's relationship so-
lidified, and they became secretly engaged. "Secret,
to the extent that the German and Japanese high com-
mands weren't aware of it," Bush wrote in *Looking
Forward*. They didn't formally announce the engage-
ment to the world until that fall in the *New York
Times*, but in the meantime their families knew.

"I do remember calling my family, saying that
George and I were engaged. The family said, 'Oh,
really?' "—which was quite a different reaction from
the one her parents had had when her sister, Martha,
had told them that she was going to marry Walter
Rafferty. Barbara always felt that Martha had broken
the ice for her. "It was so obvious to them we were
in love that of course they didn't have to be told. It
was sort of 'How could you be so silly? We've known
it all along.' " Still, Barbara would joke years later
that she had "hurt feelings for a couple of days . . .
they could have put up a little bit of a fight."

Actually, George Bush never asked anybody for
Barbara's hand, nor did he get down on bended knee.
As she told me on that California trip in the spring
of 1988: "Did he ask me if he could run for president?
The answer is no, but he didn't 'ask' me to marry
him either."

George finished his training at the Naval Air Station in Charlestown, Rhode Island, about that time
and was assigned to VT-51, a torpedo squadron that
was sent to the Pacific. Meanwhile Barbara Pierce,
who would one day follow Nancy Davis Reagan into
the White House, also followed her onto the campus

at Smith College in Northampton, Massachusetts. Their paths never crossed, however, since Nancy graduated in June 1943 and Barbara entered as a freshman that September. She lived at Tyler House, and like everyone else got around the sprawling campus either on foot or by bicycle. Always a solidly female scene, Smith was even without its usual male quotient from nearby Ivy League schools because of the war. Smithys spent Saturday nights at the movies, wrote letters to their beaus in far-flung military posts, and with a certain foreboding, read the weekly casualty list in the *New York Times*.

Barbara captained the class of 1947 soccer team, was "very social," and paid scant attention to her studies. By her own admission, she was a "lousy" student who much preferred to think about George Bush, off in the South Pacific. At the height of the 1988 campaign when George's running mate was under criticism for his undistinguished record in college, Barbara reviewed her own college record. "I didn't like to study very much," she told an interviewer. "I was thinking about Dan Quayle—I'd hate to have anybody go through my records from freshman year. I was all right in high school, but when it came to Smith, I was a cliffhanger. The truth is, I just wasn't very interested. I was just interested in George."

Barbara dropped out of Smith in 1944, at the beginning of her sophomore year. That September, Bush's plane, a Grumman Avenger he had named *Barbara*, was hit by flack in a raid on Chichi Jima. The torpedo bomber went into a dive, but Bush managed to drop its four 500-pound bombs and fly out to sea. He told his two crewmen to bail out and jumped himself shortly after that. He never again saw radioman Jack Delaney and gunnery officer William G. White, a friend from home who had been a last-minute addition to the crew. George, too, might have died had not squadron mates spotted him and kept the Japanese at bay so he could swim to his seatback rubber raft, floating some distance away. Rescued by an American submarine in the area, George rejoined his squadron two months later. He suffered a gashed forehead and was awarded the Distinguished Flying Cross for completing the mission on Chichi Jima.

At home, Barbara, planning a December 19 wedding, was unaware of what had happened; she thought he was "happily flying away," as she put it. Prescott and Dorothy Bush heard from a friend of George's that he had been shot down, but they kept from Barbara the fact that he was missing. She was grateful for that, she said later. She only knew about it three or four days before George got word to her and his family that he was safe. He was twenty years old and a veteran of fifty-eight combat missions when he arrived home on Christmas Eve. Hollywood could not have written a better script. As he described it in his book, "there were tears, laughs, hugs, joy, the love and warmth of family in a holiday setting."

On January 6, 1945, nineteen days later than they had originally expected, Barbara Pierce, wearing Dorothy Walker Bush's veil and the long-sleeved, appliquéd, white satin gown she has kept to this day, married Lieutenant Junior Grade George Bush, in his Navy dress blues, at the First Presbyterian Church in Rye. "I married the first man I ever kissed," Barbara said years later. "When I tell this to my children, they just about throw up."

The wedding itself wasn't without drama. In the vestibule, the eight bridal attendants, dressed in emerald-green satin gowns with matching green ostrich feathers in their hair and carrying bouquets of red and white carnations, were starting the procession to the altar. Behind them, poised to follow, were Barbara and her father. Suddenly, the church door flew open and a young man in a Navy midshipman's uniform rushed in. After a hair-raising trip by rented plane from Cornell University, he had landed on a frozen lake and raced by waiting car to the church, sprinting across the lawn just as the organist sounded the first chords of the wedding march.

"Barbara knew who I was though we'd never met before, but Mr. Pierce tried to throw me out, thinking I was some drunk," remembered FitzGerald Bemiss, a childhood pal whose father was an old friend of Prescott Bush's from summers at Kennebunkport. "Barbara stripped off my coat, shoved me into the last slot in the line. Up front, George and his brother Prescott, the best man, waited, and in a stage whisper that I could hear all the way down the aisle, Pressy exclaimed, 'Bemiss!' "

Afterward, at the Apawamis Club in Rye, the newlyweds led off the dancing to the approving glances of parents, siblings, and the more than 250 guests—"mostly women and old folks" because of the war, Barbara remembered. George Bush felt no more comfortable on the dance floor than he had three years earlier. This time though there was no way he could sit it out. The adoring look he gave his bride, captured in photographs of that dance, gave no hint he'd have had it any other way.

After a honeymoon to Sea Island, Georgia, married life began with a series of moves while George was being retrained for combat duty. The couple spent nine months at military bases in Michigan, Maine, and Virginia, what Barbara called "eye-opening" months filled with fear that his squadron would be called up again and he wouldn't come back.

They were living in Virginia Beach while George was stationed at Oceana Naval Air Station in August 1945 when the electrifying news that Japan had surrendered sent everybody into the streets to celebrate, and some, like George and Barbara, into their churches to give thanks, too. By September, George was enrolled at Yale, his discharge expedited because of his months in combat and the decorations he had been awarded.

George majored in economics and Barbara majored in George. By the following spring, George was playing first base on the Yale baseball team and Barbara was watching from behind the dugout. She loved baseball. She kept score—fielder's choice, error, triple. "Not many people know how to score a baseball game," George said proudly, even years later. Eventually, the Yale coach, Ethan Allen, made her move behind home plate so she would be protected by a high wire fence—she was very pregnant. If she wanted, she could also sit in the special double seat the school created by removing one arm years earlier for another baseball fan, President William Howard Taft, who weighed about 300 pounds.

Their first child, George Walker Bush, was born July 6, 1946. Shavaun Robinson Towers, Barbara's friend from Ashley Hall and Smith who had been among her bridal attendants, went to New Haven for the christening and the lawn party afterward. "I was so awed I had a friend who had a baby," she said. Little George introduced Barbara to a world that would compete for, and at times monopolize, her energies for the next twenty years. "The only place we could find [to live] took children and no pets . . . or pets and no children. We opted for the child." Turbo, their black standard poodle, was packed off to George's parents.

The Bushes belonged to a campus coterie of young marrieds, many of whom made do on the GI Bill and what they had saved of their military pay. The Bushes never talked about money, but friends remembered them as careful about what they spent. Barbara brought home a small paycheck from the Yale Co-op, where she worked that first year. Dotsie Wheeler Adams, another young bride on campus, recalled that when Barbara once brought home some old books she had bought in a secondhand store, George told her she would have to return them because they couldn't afford to keep them. "By the time we moved from Yale I knew how to wash diapers and cook dinner," said Barbara, whose reputation for split-pea soup continued to linger in some Yalie households years later.

A joiner who had a way of rising to the top, George was president of Delta Kappa Epsilon fraternity, captain of the Yale baseball team, Phi Beta Kappa, and a member of Skull and Bones, Yale's exclusive and most secretive student club. He played on the Yale soccer team, held class positions when called upon to do so, was on the tennis court and golf course whenever he could get there, and headed the United Negro College Fund on the Yale campus. "He got me involved in the United Negro College Fund way back then," Barbara said. "I don't think anybody's ever questioned our social conscience who's known about it. . . . Both of us have worked all our lives trying to help other people, as volunteers."

Fellow Bonesman Thomas W.L. (Lud) Ashley later remembered that George had told their Skull and Bones brothers that he wasn't sure he wanted to work on Wall Street, where his uncle Herbert Walker had a stock-brokerage firm. But George didn't talk much about the plans he and Barbara had for after graduation. Jobs weren't all that easy to come by, and the tendency was to play down career ideas. "People who popped off about what they were going to do rarely brought it off," Ashley said. "We didn't talk about our life ambitions mainly because all of us had just come back from three years away and we were taking it day, month, and year at a time, getting back into a mode of life that had become a little foreign to us."

William F. Howe, Jr., a Yale friend from their Andover days whom George asked to be little George's godfather, remembered driving back to town from the Yale golf course with George's father, Prescott, an investment banker at the time, and his uncle Herbert. "George and I were in the backseat. His dad was driving and stopped for gas. In the gas station, George asked his father, 'If you were in politics, would you get out of the car now and go shake hands with everybody?' His father thought a minute then said, yes, he probably would. I thought what an interesting question to ask his father."

George and Barbara thought briefly about farming, but only briefly. In his book, Bush wrote that they had never considered asking their families for "seed money." According to Barbara, he had saved $5,000 in the Navy and had used part of it along with GI Bill money to pay for college. With $3,000 left over after he graduated in June 1948, he headed for Texas in the 1947 red Studebaker his father had given him for graduation after George's car died on the highway. Awaiting him in Odessa was a job as an equipment clerk with the International Derrick and Equipment Company (Ideco). George hadn't just picked the job out of a hat; Ideco was part of Dresser Industries, an oil conglomerate whose head, Neil Mallon, had been a Bones brother of George's father's at Yale. Through the years he had also been both "surrogate uncle" and "father-confessor" to all the

Bush offspring. It was Mallon who suggested that George return to Texas, where he had spent time in flight training before going to the Pacific. Texas had oil fields, Mallon told him, and oil was the black gold that was fueling ambition.

When George arrived, he could have counted the number of producing oil wells in the county on one hand—with a finger to spare. The big strike of 1949 was still to come. George wasn't yet in that league anyway, but neither was he without resources. Talking about their big adventure to Paul Hendrickson of the *Washington Post* in 1981, Barbara Bush gave it some perspective. "Well, I mean, George was a Phi Beta Kappa. It wasn't exactly like we were going to a foreign country. We could have come home." They could have, but they didn't.

Barbara and young George arrived about a week after George senior. She hadn't really wanted to go but realized later it was probably the best thing she ever did. "My sister had always picked out my clothes, my mother picked out my clothes, and I was perfectly willing to let Mrs. Bush, who I adore, make all my decisions," she told Marty Primeau of the *Dallas Morning News* in 1984. Pauline Pierce thought Odessa, Texas, "was like Russia" and kept sending Barbara boxes of Tide because she was certain they didn't have such a thing as soap there. "I finally had to tell her that there were plenty of grocery stores around and that it was bigger than Rye, New York."

The move away from family shaped their lives. "I think we'd have probably not grown up as quickly.

I think it was very good for our marriage," she once told me. "When you are a couple all grown up, nobody's son or daughter, nobody's shadow, you are you."

Odessa was a rough and tumble prairie town poking out of the West Texas sagebrush. People lived where they could, some in trailers, some in converted chicken coops, some—like the Bushes—in the other half of a whorehouse. The apartment in an East Seventh Street shotgun house had three beds in a row in one room, three chairs and one table in the second room, and a kitchen at the end. Two prostitutes and one little girl lived on the other side of a jerry-rigged partition. "Everything is relative in life," Barbara said later. "As we had the only bathroom on the street, we didn't complain."

George earned $300 a month, not all that bad for a young guy just starting out. They lived in Odessa less than a year before Dresser Industries sent him to California. There, George traveled a thousand miles a week as a drilling-bit salesman, moving his family with him from Huntington Park to Bakersfield to Whittier, Ventura, and Compton. In Compton, in December 1949, their second child, a daughter, was born. Barbara hadn't met the doctor before that day. Though not in the delivery room, George was there, just as he was when all their children were born.

6

No Crying Aloud

"I hadn't cried at all when Robin was alive, but after she died, I felt I could cry forever."

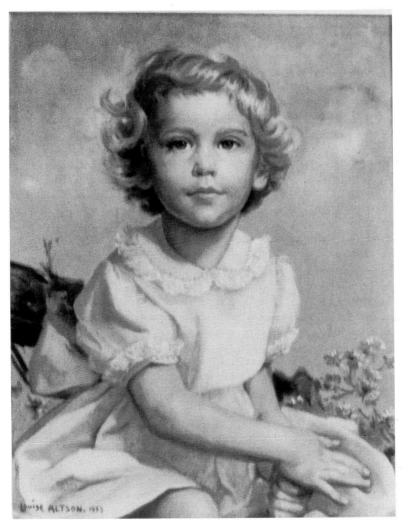

Robin, the Bushes' daughter who died of leukemia at age three. Through her illness and death, George and Barbara drew their strength from friends, faith, and each other. (*Bush Family Album*)

George and Barbara in Texas with their four sons. (*Bush Family Album*)

Houston, 1959. George holds baby Dorothy—"Doro." (*Bush Family Album*)

The Bush family in Texas in the mid-sixties. (*Bush Family Album*)

George and Barbara on election night in 1966, when he becomes the first Republican to win a House seat in Harris County, Texas. (*Bush Family Album*)

By 1969, President Richard Nixon was urging George to run for the Senate and helped by making this campaign appearance in Dallas, Texas, on October 28, 1970. George lost to Lloyd Bentsen, Jr., 53.4 to 46.6 percent. (*Courtesy Nixon Project, National Archives*)

President Nixon helped George again, appointing him to the post of UN Representative. Here, he is being sworn in on February 26, 1971, surrounded by (*left to right*) his neighbor and friend Associate Justice Potter Stewart, Barbara, and Nixon. (*Courtesy Nixon Project, National Archives*)

A good day for tennis at the Kennebunk River Club in Kennebunkport, Maine, in August 1971. *Left to right*: George, Barbara, close friend Willard "Spike" Heminway, and Jodie Bush (wife of George's brother Jonathan Bush). (*Courtesy "Spike" and Betsy Heminway*)

George and Barbara bicycling in Beijing during his 1974–75 post there heading the 226-member staff at the U.S. Liaison Office. Barbara later characterized this time as "a whole new leaf in both our lives. We studied together and shared everything." (*The White House*)

Left to right: George, Susan Ford, First Lady Betty Ford, Barbara, President Gerald Ford in the courtyard of the U.S. Liaison Office in Beijing on December 4, 1975, shortly before the Bushes returned to the United States. (*Courtesy Gerald R. Ford Library*)

By the time Barbara reached the White House in January 1989, she was the most widely traveled wife of any American president, having accompanied George to sixty-eight countries on trips totaling 1,330,239 miles. Here, she enjoys a sunny day with George in front of the Taj Mahal on May 13, 1984. (*David Valdez/The White House*)

George and Barbara tour the Cairo pyramids during an official trip to Israel, Jordan, and Egypt in August 1986. (*David Valdez/The White House*)

George looks on while Barbara holds a cub in Niger's National Culture Museum, on March 8, 1985. They were on the second leg of a three-country African tour. (*UPI/Bettmann Newsphotos*)

Left to right: George, Mrs. Hannelore Kohl, Barbara, and West German Chancellor Helmut Kohl on June 25, 1985. (*David Valdez/ The White House*)

George and Barbara with Denis Thatcher and British Prime Minister Margaret Thatcher, February 12, 1984. As the Second Lady, Barbara enjoyed her anonymity while traveling. In those days, she went virtually unnoticed by the ubiquitous press. (*David Valdez/The White House*)

In September 1987, the Bushes somberly tour the site of a Nazi concentration camp at Auschwitz, Poland. (*David Valdez/The White House*)

*T*hey named her Pauline Robinson Bush, after Barbara's mother, who had been killed in an automobile accident two months earlier. They called her Robin, as full of life and promise as the bird that comes with springtime. She was blond with hazel eyes and as perfect a baby as any parent could want.

Pauline Pierce's death had been so freakish. She had taken a cup of coffee along when she and Marvin left the house on an October morning in 1949, and as they drove, she set the cup on the seat beside her. Marvin saw it starting to slide and fearing Pauline would be scalded, tried to stop it. He lost control of the car and hit a stone wall. Marvin was hospitalized with several broken ribs and facial contusions; Pauline died instantly. Barbara didn't go to the funeral. On the phone, Marvin urged her to stay where she was. With the baby due so soon, he worried that the trip would be too hard on her and he didn't want her to take any chances. "Contrary to popular belief, it would have been an enormous financial strain," Barbara said. "My father would have had to pay for my trip. But he would have."

The Bushes moved back to Texas soon after. Not to Odessa but to Midland, another former cow town down the road where the oil boom was on. They bought a blue house on East Maple Street in a pastel-colored neighborhood that everybody called Easter Egg Row. The price tag was $7,500 and for that they got 847 square feet but no dining room. "Guests just kind of ate on their laps," remembered Dorothy Craig, a friend from those days. They did get their own backyard though. That yard wasn't just where they sent the kids to play; it became the backbone of their social life.

Everybody was from someplace else, and nobody had families other than the ones they were building. So friends became surrogate relatives, extended families that barbecued hamburgers and played touch football together on Sundays while their kids rode their tricycles, fell off their swings, and cried when their dogs licked their faces. Children were what people who used to live there remembered best about the

Midland of the fifties. Everybody had four, five, six, some even eight—like C. Fred and Marion Chambers, two of the Bushes' best friends. "We finally decided it was the water," said Marion. When the doctor said her fifth was on the way, she drove over to see Barbara. "I told her I had thought I had a tumor but that the doctor said 'the tumor has arms and legs.' Bar started crying. I said, 'I'm the one who should be crying.' "

In Barbara's memory "it was just the right time to live there. I remember Dad visiting us in Midland and saying, 'I worry about you. What if something happened? Who would support you?' Well, we were all in the same situation. No one had any family. We were all newcomers and we came from all over the country. We formed really good friendships."

Barbara tended to the needs of George W. and Robin, while big George and their across-the-street neighbor, John Overbey, started their own oil business. There were civic obligations as well. George helped start the YMCA and raise funds for the Little Theater and the United Fund, and he wasn't yet thirty when he became a director of a bank. As a family, they went to the Presbyterian Church. As a couple, they taught Sunday school.

Barbara's life was comfortable without glamour. "There were very dormant years in there where I was perfectly happy to have children. I always did volunteer work, but I didn't do anything imaginative or creative. George was building businesses all around the world, and we couldn't afford for me to go to those places with him." It was a time when fewer than one-third of America's married women with school-age children worked outside the home. As a schoolgirl, Barbara had never had any serious career ambitions. Her first and—except for the year she worked at the Yale Co-op—her only job was when she was sixteen, the first summer after World War II started. Like Americans of all ages not in uniform and eager to do their patriotic duty, Barbara wanted to help in the war effort. She went to work for a nuts and bolts factory in Port Chester, New York. Years later, the closest she came to fulfilling a career ambition was as a hospital and nursing home volunteer. "I think I wanted to be a nurse," she said. But she was not a complainer. "There's a time. A time for babies, a time for growing. I just happened to lie dormant in rather important years, and I might regret that. But I don't think so," she told the *Dallas Morning News* in 1984.

Then one early-spring day in 1953, shortly after John Ellis Bush (Jeb) was born, Robin, who was three, told Barbara that she just couldn't decide what to do that day. "I'm either going to lie on the bed and look at books or lie in the grass and watch cars go by," Robin said. Barbara was bewildered. She saw no reason why her little girl, outwardly looking so normal—"I wasn't observant enough to notice that she had some small bruises on her legs"—would be so listless, but she was determined to find out. She took Robin to the children's pediatrician, Dr. Dorothy Wyvell, who examined her, took a blood test, then asked Barbara to come back that afternoon with George.

Frightened by now, Barbara phoned George, who was about twenty miles away, at the Ector County courthouse checking over land records for the Bush-Overbey Oil Development Company. Together at the doctor's office, they heard Dr. Wyvell tell them that Robin had leukemia. Leukemia? They had never heard of it. What could they do to make Robin well? Dr. Wyvell, a family friend as well as the children's doctor, dabbed at her tears. There was nothing they could do, she told them. Robin's illness was so advanced—her white-blood-cell count was the highest the doctor had ever seen—that she had very little time left to live.

"Then she gave us the best advice anyone could have given, which of course we didn't take," Barbara said in a 1988 interview with Amy Cunningham of *Texas Monthly.* "She said, 'Number one, don't tell anyone. Number two, don't treat her. You should take her home, make life as easy as possible for her, and in three weeks' time, she'll be gone.' "

By evening everyone in the neighborhood knew, and George and Barbara were surrounded by their surrogate family offering support. The next day they flew to New York, where George's uncle, Dr. John Walker, a former cancer specialist who was president of New York's Memorial Hospital, had urged they consult specialists with the Sloan-Kettering Foundation. "You could never live with yourselves unless you treat her," he told them.

Robin was given a cancer drug that researchers had developed a year earlier. She responded well, though there was never a total remission. For years afterward Dr. Charlotte Tan, a pediatrician and one of the physicians working with the child, remembered her spunk and maturity. "It takes a really big girl to tolerate an oxygen tent and all that when you're three years old."

For seven months, Barbara hardly left Robin's side, whether at her hospital bed in New York or back in Texas during those times she was better, when it was difficult to think of her as dying. Once George took her with him to the bank, walking there from his office. "They said, 'Where's the little girl who was so sick?' And here she was, she looked so beautiful —just like she was at the peak of her life," George said.

He drew strength from church, where he stopped to pray on his way to work in the morning. Their friends did what they could to help, giving blood to replace that used for the transfusions that Robin needed all too frequently. At home, fearing Robin might be bruised, Barbara refused to let her and young George play together. "We thought he was too young to know, and actually I didn't want Robin to know. . . . I made up my mind that she was going to be happy."

Robin was brave. She didn't know she was going to die, though she knew she was pretty sick. Barbara read to her all day long, tickled her, and loved her, and Robin was young enough that she didn't think ahead, which was merciful for Barbara and George. The child was "one dimensional," said Barbara. "It made it a little bit easier. She never said, 'When I grow up, I want to be . . . ,' which would have been hard for us." It was hard enough as it was. Barbara wouldn't allow anybody to cry in Robin's room. The worst offenders were George and his mother, Dorothy Bush, who were so softhearted.

"Midland was wonderful," Barbara said. "They all rallied around—the church and friends. It was an interesting time for me because some of my best friends, people I'd seen all the time, really couldn't cope with Robin's sickness. Some of the people I knew only fairly well, like Betty Liedtke, whose husband was in business with George, never left my side. It was the most amazing thing. And when I brought Robin home, it was so scary because she'd hemorrhage and didn't eat and Betty was there every day with some wonderful food because if Robin didn't eat, we'd have to go back to New York."

All this time George W., who was seven, and Jeb, only a few months, were needing love, too. When Barbara was home, she gave what she had, but when she and Robin were in New York, George had to try to be both mother and father. He couldn't be away from his business all the time, but he flew to New York on weekends, leaving George W. and Jeb with neighbors. Eventually Dorothy Bush sent a nurse down to help George with the children. In New York, doing what he could to comfort his little girl —holding her when she had pneumonia, helping her do such a simple thing as blow her nose—George watched her condition deteriorate and he suffered. "He was just killing himself, while I was very strong," Barbara said.

"I remember asking the doctor why this was happening to our little girl, this perfectly beautiful creature," Barbara said. "And the doctor said, 'You have to realize that every well person is a miracle. It takes billions of cells to make up a person. And all it takes is one cell to be bad to destroy a whole person.' So I came to see that the people who are sitting around alive are the miracles."

When Robin slept, Barbara walked the halls at Sloan-Kettering. She listened to the staff, talked to the children, met their parents, and shared some of their sorrows. Or sometimes, from a forty-second-floor window, she'd just gaze at the Manhattan skyline. Lud Ashley, their friend from Yale who was living in New York at the time, knew to look for her there. "I never saw her cry. It was one of the wonders," said Ashley, for whom there was never any question that this was one of the really remarkable women he was ever going to know.

Then one day in October, Robin started to hemorrhage. George was on his way up from Texas, but Barbara was alone. Robin was such a frail little thing by then, her skin almost transparent over her wasted bones. The bleeding might be stopped but there could never be any lasting reprieve from the end that surely was coming. Barbara, who was twenty-eight at the time, stuck out her jaw and stood very firm.

"Robin was in remission but she had holes all through her tummy. Our uncle-doctor, whom we love more than life, really thought we ought to let her go. The doctors at Memorial really wanted to operate—they knew so little about all that. I opted to go with the doctors." And then, talking to me thirty-six years later at the White House, Barbara started to cry. "She was very, very sick. She never came out of the operation. But they asked me to do it. Although Johnny Walker [the uncle], to spare us, said you don't have to do that, I just felt they were killing themselves to save a child and we ought to cooperate. I don't care what anybody says, where there's life there's hope."

When George arrived, he knew Barbara had been right. When Robin died, they both were with her. "You learn how people react—Barbara's strength, and then I saw other families that reacted very differently," George told me in 1988 at Kennebunkport a few days before the Republican Convention. "We saw one group—their child had just died—and they were asked for permission to do an autopsy and they turned on the nurses and doctors, saying, 'Haven't you done enough?' They were so grief-stricken they turned on the people who helped them the most. Barbara's and my reaction was very different from that. I think we love everyone more because of Robin."

The next day, George went back to the hospital to thank everyone who had helped their child. What he could not know, according to Ashley, was that among the staff were people "crying like hell" because Robin's death also meant saying good-bye to Barbara. As Barbara described that day, she and George just got up and went to Rye, where they played golf with her father and didn't tell anyone what had happened. "I remember seeing people there in the locker room —I always felt sort of guilty about it—but I never said a word and I know they read it in the paper [and probably thought] 'Gosh, how insensitive.' But that was my way.

"I just fell apart when she died. I said, 'George, I just can't go downstairs.' There were all those people down there. And he looked out the window and saw my darling sister coming up the driveway with her husband—her name is Martha Rafferty—and he joked, 'Here are the O'Raffertys. It's going to be a hell of a wake.' And somehow or other, it made it better. . . . If it wasn't for that, I would not have gotten down those damn stairs.

"We gave Robin's body to Sloan-Kettering and said do with it what you will. About three months after her death they let me know her liver had died. Sort of insensitive, except we were into research." George had set up a foundation called Bright Star Foundation, and the Bushes have signed to donate their own organs. "Well, what do I want them for? I don't feel squeamish about that," Barbara explained in 1989. "I don't think I've got anything that's useful, but anything I've got, they can use it for research as far as I'm concerned.

"Robin we donated to research because she was

gone. But I would hope I've got the courage again to give whatever anyone needed. I hope I would. Or the heart, not the courage. We were with Robin—I was with her, awake when she was born, and I was with her when she died. She was the only child I've seen come to life. And first of all, I know there's a God, and secondly, I know Robin left. We both had that feeling that she wasn't there. We combed her hair and she wasn't there."

Lud Ashley and Dorothy Bush buried Robin later. At one point when she was still alive, George's father, Prescott, by then a U.S. senator from Connecticut, had asked Barbara if she would come out and help him, under the pretext of picking out his own gravesite. "He and I went out. I remember distinctly a big mausoleum that had 'Hall' written on it. He said, 'I don't see myself as Mr. Hall. I see myself as Bush.' And so we picked a lovely little spot. He put a bush up, a lovely hedge and tree. He said, 'Now, I'll be very comfortable.' He did that for Robin," Barbara said, then finished, "He's there, too, now."

George and Barbara went back to Texas, where the pain became physical, "like our hearts were breaking," Barbara said. At home, she surrendered to her sorrow. "I hadn't cried at all when Robin was alive," Barbara said in the *Texas Monthly* interview, "but after she died, I felt I could cry forever."

What saved her were her two Georges. Young George did so unknowingly. He was only seven at the time, but grieving, too; he had felt cheated by Robin's death and could not believe she was buried.

"One time he asked me if she was buried this way" —vertically—"or this way"—horizontally. I said, 'Well, what difference would it make?' He said, 'Well, one way she'd be spinning around like this, one way like this.' " Barbara devoted much of her time to playing with him and baby Jeb, and Georgie humored her. "One day I heard Georgie tell a friend, 'I can't play today because I have to be with my mother— she's so unhappy.' That's when I realized you either pull together or you shatter," she said.

The other George refused to let her retreat into her grief. "He just didn't let me misbehave. People came by to see me all the time. He never let me be alone. He was so funny. He'd take Georgie places and he'd come back and tell me what Georgie said. He'd go to a football game and young George would say, 'Wish I was Robin.' George said all the men with him would just freeze up. Nobody mentioned her. George said, 'Well, why, George?' 'Well, she has a better seat than we do!' George kept me laughing with wonderful stories."

Years later she sometimes cited statistics that "seventy percent of the people who lose children get divorced because one doesn't talk to the other. He did not allow that." As Robin lay dying, he had suffered and Barbara had been strong. Now the opposite was true. That was the way "a good marriage works," she said. "Had I cried a lot, he wouldn't have. But things reversed after she died. George seemed to accept it better."

At the Republican National Convention in New

Orleans in August 1988, Barbara told it this way to 2,300 delegates: "He held me in his arms, and he made me share it, and accept that his sorrow was as great as my own. He simply wouldn't allow my grief to divide us . . . push us apart, which is what happens so often where there is a loss like that. And for as long as I live, I will respect and appreciate my husband for the strength of his understanding."

For Bush, Robin's death had done something more than draw them together. "You learn what faith is," he told me at Kennebunkport.

For Barbara, too, even enduring what seemed like interminable agony those days and nights at the hospital, not everything could be considered negative. "We looked around and nobody had what we had. They either didn't believe in God or they didn't love each other or they didn't have other children or they didn't have brothers and sisters. In a way it was good for us because we realized we had much more than anybody else," she told the *Houston Post*'s Kathy Lewis in 1986 when the Bushes returned to Sloan-Kettering to break ground for a new research laboratory.

"You know, I consider Robin a happy experience," Barbara could say by 1989. "I don't mind talking about her. I cry when I'm happy."

"If the ending would have been different," George told the *New York Times*' Gerald Boyd that same year, "it would have been the greatest experience of our lives."

7

Ties That Bind

"If I didn't agree with George on something the children were supposed to do, we talked about it in private and came out with a united front. . . . That's the way you bring up well-behaved children."

*B*arbara had always wanted a big family. "I'm speaking about me. I don't know about George," she said, laughing, when I asked them about that at Walker's Point, the Bush family home in Kennebunkport. "Did you want to have a big family?" she asked, turning to watch him. "Too late to ask you now."

"Sure," said George, looking a little uncomfortable, then gesturing toward the Bush tribe that had gathered for the last big preconvention family convocation. "And we do. You've seen them all."

Kennebunkport was where Prescott and Dorothy Bush's family had always been the closest and happiest. Every summer when George Bush was growing up, his parents put kids and dogs into the car and drove from Greenwich to Walker's Point, named for her father and grandfather, who had bought it jointly. For a couple of summers years later, Barbara piled her kids and dogs into a station wagon and drove them from Midland to the same house. Dorothy Bush would tell her, "You cannot do this, Bar," and Barbara would say, "Don't be silly, Mother." But Dorothy Bush was always impressed with the pioneer spirit in her daughter-in-law, that "there was no moaning or groaning or hiring someone to drive the car. Barbara just got in and drove it," Nancy Ellis said.

The loss of Robin had left a seven-year gap between her firstborn, George W., and Jeb. But the other children arrived with some regularity: Neil Mallon Bush (1955), named for Neil Mallon, who had pointed George Bush toward Texas in 1948; Marvin Pierce Bush (1956), named for Barbara's father; and Dorothy (Doro) Walker Bush (1959), named for George's mother.

By her own description, Barbara was the "traditional, supportive mother." By George's description that August day in Kennebunkport: "Barbara always went the extra mile—every inning of their Little League game or every tear to be wiped away, every broken heart later on in some young romance."

If down in Midland she sometimes resembled the sitcom heroines of the 1950s, those perfect homemakers whose houses were spotless, children precious, and husbands dauntless as they worked toward the great American dream, it did not surprise her friends. She was highly organized. Her cupboards were stocked, her children's scrapbooks up-to-date, her thank-you notes always in the mail. She methodically sewed nametags in her children's clothes and cooked commendable spaghetti. She never missed a meeting with the teachers and never played bridge. Her housekeeping matched her mind: no clutter.

"She always made me feel like a slob," said Marion Chambers.

In her 1985 speech at American University's Distinguished Lecture series conducted by Jihan el Sadat, the widow of Egyptian president Anwar Sadat, Barbara told it this way:

"This was a period, for me, of long days and short years; of diapers, runny noses, earaches, more Little League games than you could believe possible, tonsils, and those unscheduled races to the hospital emergency room, Sunday School and church, of hours of urging homework, short chubby arms around your neck and sticky kisses; and experiencing bumpy moments—not many, but a few—of feeling that I'd never, ever be able to have fun again; and coping with the feeling that George Bush, in his excitement of starting a small company and traveling around the world, was having a lot of fun."

As an independent oilman and his own boss, George was away from home far more than he had ever been as a salaried salesman. When he wasn't trying to buy some landowner's mineral rights, he was back East trying to line up investors. His efforts had their rewards; the Bushes were the first of their Midland crowd to have a swimming pool.

"I had moments where I was jealous of attractive young women, out in a man's world," Barbara said later. "I would think, well, George is off on a trip doing all these exciting things and I'm sitting home with these absolutely brilliant children, who say one thing a week of interest."

If she gave any thought to choosing a profession, it was nursing, she once said. But in those early Texas years somebody had to take care of the nest. "And that's me," said Barbara, who pulled double duty as mother and father throughout most of the fifties. Talking about that role three decades later, she belittled her importance. "In a marriage where one is so willing to take on responsibility and the other so willing to keep the bathrooms clean, that's the way you get treated," she told Diane Casselberry Manuel of the *Christian Science Monitor*. "Whenever there were any big decisions, the children always went to their father, probably because they'd always seen me as the—I hate to say 'laundress'—but as the nagging mother who said, 'Have you done your homework?' "

Her children didn't remember it quite that way. "Even when we were growing up in Houston, Dad wasn't home at night to play catch. Mom was always the one to hand out the goodies and the discipline. In a sense, it was a matriarchal family," Jeb Bush told an interviewer during his father's 1980 campaign for president. Nine years later Jeb said he never did figure out how his mother had juggled it all. "Maybe there were two of her," he joked to me. "My dad was hardly around. It was pretty remarkable how everybody got attention. We were all encouraged to be involved in extracurricular activities. She had to handle all this stuff. . . . Barbara Bush reincarnated as a young woman in the 1980s or '90s would be the chief executive officer of a major corporation."

Jeb couldn't recall her ever losing her temper either. Said George W.: "My mother's always been a very outspoken person who vents very well—she'll just let it rip if she's got something on her mind. Once it's over, you know exactly where you stand and that's it. She doesn't dwell on it or hound you or anything like that."

Soft on the inside, tough on the outside, and always consistent, Barbara was the day-to-day disciplinarian whose word was law and punishment swift. "She let us know when we crossed the line, and the line never shifted," said Jeb. "She'd say, 'All right, this is the way we're going to do it or you go to your room,' " said Doro. "She's understanding, she'd listen to reason, but somebody had to set the guidelines, otherwise there's chaos. She was the one who did that."

And George Bush, remembered by the daughter he adored as soft on the inside *and* outside? "He'd get in on it every once in a while," said Doro, who conceded that as the only girl she had an advantage. Mostly though, his children knew George as the ultimate authority who only stepped in when war broke out. Even then, his was a position more figurative than corporeal. "When he came home, he didn't have to be the disciplinarian," said Jeb.

If George and Barbara had disagreements over family rules, they didn't let their children know it. "If I didn't agree with George on something the children were supposed to do, we talked about it in private and came out with a united front. That's the way you ought to do in married life. That's the way you bring up well-behaved children," Barbara said. The only time George W. remembered one parent overruling the other was when Barbara found out he smoked. "I was eighteen or nineteen at the time and she got upset and told me I shouldn't smoke. I remember my father clearly saying, 'Barbara, who are you to tell your son he shouldn't smoke as you so deeply inhale your Newport?' I guess she stopped smoking when she saw all her kids start."

Barbara made light of her role as the disciplinarian years later. "I remember I called George one day when the boys were small and I said, 'I'm desperate—I don't know what to do. Your son's in trouble again. He just hit a ball through the neighbor's upstairs window.' And George said, 'Wow. What a great hit!' And then he said, 'Did you get the ball back?' "

At Kennebunkport that day with me, she said he gave the children more independence than she did. "And in retrospect, I now think he was right. He trusted them a little more than I did, and I think that gave them a lot of—"

"Elbowroom, headroom," finished George.

"You ask them and they would tell you that his worst side was he listened to every side of every argument and never gave them advice, let them think it out for themselves," Barbara continued. "They might say it was his most frustrating habit, only because a couple of times they really wanted advice, they really wanted him to say, 'I think you ought to do this.' "

"In Dad's case he never really tried to direct your life," George W. said. About the worst his children could expect from George Bush was for him to tell them he was "disappointed" in something they did. That was his reaction upon learning that because George W. missed his girlfriend and wanted to be with her before they both returned to college, he had quit his job roughnecking on an offshore oil rig before he had fulfilled his commitment to his employer. "Before long I was called to my father's office in downtown Houston," George W. remembered. "He simply told me: 'In our family, and in life, you fulfill your commitments; you've disappointed me'—and that was it." Three hours later Bush took his son and his girlfriend to the Houston Astros game. "Which says a lot about him and how he disciplines," George W. told CBS talk-show host Charlie Rose shortly before the 1988 convention.

George Herbert Walker Bush was the second of

five children of Prescott and Dorothy Bush, whose formula for child-rearing had included "generous measures of both love and discipline," daily Bible lessons, and church on Sunday. "Dad taught us about duty and service. Mother taught us about dealing with life on a personal basis, relating to other people," George wrote in *Looking Forward*, which he dedicated to his parents "whose values lit the way."

No small part of those values was the importance Dorothy Bush placed on sportsmanship, the underlying code by which she reared her family. She was an accomplished athlete from a family of accomplished athletes. "His mother was the most competitive living human," said Barbara. Nancy Ellis remembered home as a place where for years the Ping-Pong table stood in the front hall and guests coming to dinner just had to step around it. But though Dorothy Bush wanted her children to win the game, according to Barbara, "the way you played it was much more important. If you didn't play it the right way, with fairness, courtesy, and decency, she threw you off the court or the links or whatever she was on."

Dorothy Bush once said her policy and that of her husband was to let their children do "whatever they strongly wished." There were, of course, limitations on one's behavior. "If you scaled your racket across the court, you were history," George Bush told George Plimpton for *Sports Illustrated* in 1988. And when ten-year-old George ordered his aunt Mary Walker off the premises for laughing during a Kennebunkport tournament in which he was a finalist, his mother made him apologize for such rudeness. Justice prevailed in another way as well. George lost the match. "It must have bothered my conscience," he told Plimpton. Another Dorothy Bush call, famous within the family, was made after George, playing mixed doubles with Barbara on the Kennebunkport court, ran into a porch and injured his right shoulder blade. "His mother said it was my ball to hit, and it happened because I didn't run for it. She was probably right," Barbara told Plimpton.

Dorothy Bush, who believed you never gave in to the game of life, judged people by their tennis. When a discussion of someone's game came up, as Barbara described it, "if Mrs. Bush would say, 'She had some good shots,' it meant she stank. That's just the way she got the message across. When one of the grandchildren brought this girl home, everybody said, 'We think he's going to marry her,' and she said, 'Oh, no, she won't play net.' He did, though, and they've been very happy ever since," negligent net game presumably notwithstanding.

But Barbara's childhood zest for tennis served her well in the Bush family. She was always active in the sports life of her own children when they were growing up, and later in that of her grandchildren, taking them to tennis clinics summers in Kennebunkport much as she had gone to in Manursing Island when she was a child. But by 1989 she had nothing to say about how she was rated by that mysterious Bush family sports institution called the Ranking Committee.

Jeb Bush, rumored to be a committee official, once tried to explain it:

"It's a mythical committee—maybe it isn't mythical, there's always the possibility that it's real, but I think it's mythical—that deals with how you work your way up the ladder. If you're not up to the level of playing whatever sport's involved, then the Ranking Committee will just let you know that you can't challenge up until you work your way up the ladder. It's been in existence for a while, at least five years, but there's never been a public meeting, and whenever they meet, it's always overnight and long distance. It could be like the Skull and Bones. I don't know."

Jeb, known to be fiercely competitive, was eventually ranked second to his brother Marvin. "I don't worry about that anymore. I play with my dad. If I'm forced to, I'll play with my mother," whom he described as "a plodder" though no slouch as a competitor. His own son, George P., was equally competitive and at the age of ten challenged his grandmother.

"He jumped to a five–nothing lead, then couldn't close. She came back and won. There were tears and rackets thrown, and my mother had to preside over this, mark it down as a learning experience. It shows that she's the kind of competitor who didn't let him win. She went for the jugular there."

After forty plus years as Dorothy Bush's daughter-in-law Barbara could hardly have done anything else. She remembered the trouncing Dorothy Bush gave her on another court during one trip to New York when Robin was sick. "She and I were alone, so we went over to play paddle tennis. Now, I had not played paddle tennis and she was the national runner-up tennis champion at seventeen. And she beat me right-handed, so then she gave me twenty–love to start with, and then she played me left-handed and beat me, and that I think is unforgivable!" said Barbara, still amused at the way Mrs. Bush had managed to take her mind off Robin. "She's the most supportive, wonderful, loving—she just was the perfect mother and the greatest mother-in-law."

In fact, Barbara was more comfortable with Dorothy Bush than she had ever been with her mother. "And that of course is not something I'm terribly proud of, but that's a sort of chemical thing." Nancy Ellis said the affection worked both ways. "Mother adored Barbara—adored all her daughters-in-law. She was forever pointing out how wonderful they were, which I took rather personally at times. You want your own mother to love you, and then love the daughters-in-law a little bit less."

Dorothy Bush made every single one of her daughters-in-law think each was her favorite person in the world. "Of course, I believed that, when she acted that way about me," said Barbara. "She would say things like 'Now, Bar, do me the biggest favor. Would you call such and such a daughter-in-law and just tell her how after breakfast you soak the dishes while you go and make the bed?' I said, 'No, I'm not going to go tell so-and-so that.' "

Dorothy Bush never criticized, never took anybody's side, according to Barbara, but she didn't have to. "Looking right at George, she would say, 'Sandy [Nancy's husband]—the most wonderful husband—always hangs his wet tennis clothes up so Nancy doesn't have to bother with that.' We'd all say, 'You mean he *wears* those dirty tennis clothes again?' " Barbara said her mother-in-law always had "this positive way" of pointing out the good points her other kids seemed to lack. "George is such a good father, he helps bathe the children," she'd say to another child who apparently didn't scrub his offspring.

"I remember that Mildred Kerr and I used to sit in Houston talking. We had all these boys between us. We'd think, 'We've just got to copy Mrs. Bush and be that kind of mother-in-law somehow or other.' " And just as Dorothy Bush had, Barbara Bush always seemed to think of her four daughters-in-law as her own daughters. It was as though she'd picked up the trait from her mother-in-law.

If there were similarities between Dorothy Bush and Barbara Bush—their unyielding grit, for instance—George W. Bush said their styles were totally different. "My grandmother is an unbelievable person, one of the most gentle, kind souls I've ever met. I wouldn't necessarily describe mother right now as a gentle soul."

Barbara's children remember her for her opinions, not her wit, though they absorbed something of her irreverent humor and teasing manner. Much as her mother had been the butt of her children's jokes,

Barbara was sometimes the butt of hers. "We tried to be disrespectful on a regular basis," said Marvin. "Out of disrespect we called her the Gray Fox." "We thought her gray hair was funny," said Doro. There were limits, however. "The biggest crime we could commit growing up was to be malicious toward someone else—finding a vulnerable spot, make fun," said Marvin.

There were other rules. Living under the Bush roof meant going to church on Sundays, abiding by family curfews, and getting a girl home by eleven P.M., even if it was a tip-off—a possibly humiliating one—that a Bush boy was expected home before his date was.

Not that any of them was perfect. "If you have three older brothers, you're not dealing with a handful of saints," admitted Marvin.

"By the time I was sixteen years old I knew what was expected of me by my parents, and it didn't take much for me to realize when I was not meeting those expectations," said Jeb. "And it didn't take lectures, though I'm sure from time to time they occurred. It was more just knowing that there was a standard expected and that anything else would be a disappointment to them. They weren't exceedingly tough standards to meet, just kind of basic right-and-wrong things. They gave us enough rope to hang ourselves without killing ourselves."

George and Barbara were no more immune than other parents to the challenge of America's youth's rebelling against prevailing standards of morality and traditions. The Bushes did not condone insubordination, but neither did they forbid freedom of expression. "They did encourage us not to assume that the status quo is the way to be—don't just get along but go do something about it," said Jeb. "And that was equal parts—both George and Barbara Bush."

The late 1960s and early 1970s carried America's young into all the turbulence engendered by Vietnam, experimental drugs, and Watergate. On a personal level, the Bush sons faced the defeat of their father in his second try for the U.S. Senate. "I mean, people were very cynical, rebelling was the 'in' thing. Without breaking any trust, I can say that the environment in which we were teenagers wasn't easy," Jeb, who had been at Andover then, told me in 1989. "The school was rebelling against itself," he told David Maraniss of the *Washington Post*. "Our class particularly. I think the school hit bottom with us. I wasn't a model citizen, nor were any of us. But it wasn't a reflection on us so much as the times."

According to Barbara, Jeb tossed around the idea of being drafted or resisting and taking the consequences. "He came down on the side of being drafted—we kidded him that we'd back him whatever," said Barbara. Jeb was never drafted. The lesson she learned that time, she said, was "to trust your children to do the right thing."

After graduating from Yale in 1968, George W. had gone into the Texas Air National Guard, a fact Barbara recalled at the height of the furor over her husband's selection of Senator Dan Quayle as his running mate in 1988. Her reaction may have provided a clue as to why George Bush saw nothing wrong with Quayle's record of military service during the Vietnam War era. Quayle came under criticism following published reports that he used family influence to gain a slot in the Indiana National Guard in 1969 as a means of avoiding the draft. A few weeks before the 1988 presidential election, Barbara was outraged that Quayle, a year younger than her son George W., was under attack. "What was wrong with that?" she asked when the question of Quayle's National Guard duty was raised. "Lloyd Bentsen's son was in the National Guard. George Bush's son was in the National Guard. And we're damn proud of him."

Nancy Ellis, living in Boston, remembered what a "rotten time the Watergate time" had been for her nephew George W. as a student at Harvard Business School. "You know Harvard Square and how they felt about Nixon. But here was Georgie, his father head of the Republican National Committee. So he came out a lot with us just to get out of there."

"There were a lot of contradictions out there," said George Bush of that time, speaking now from the Walker's Point rock wall.

"Hopelessness," said Barbara.

"A lot of difficulty for young people," George continued. "And they were schooled by people telling them our country was wrong in Vietnam. And yet they went to school, made friends, and came home.

I'm sure they had problems in their lives, but they recognized early on that the family was close, and all of them just stayed a very integral part of it."

In fact, the Bushes were almost a storybook example of the American family whose members were so much a part of each other's lives that even after they left home they continued to return regularly for weekends, for holidays, for Sunday dinner. As daughter Doro LeBlond put it: "To this day I want to come home—my whole family feels that way."

In an imaginary interview with himself in *Looking Forward*, Geoge Bush wrote:

> Q: Last question. Going back to 1948, the year you left college and went out to Texas. Out of all the things you've done since then—in business, Congress, the UN, China, the CIA, the vice presidency—what single accomplishment are you proudest of?
>
> GB: The fact that our children still come home.

"One reason we came home was the atmosphere was comfortable and warm," said George W. "Another reason we came home is the way we were raised. I've never heard George and Barbara Bush utter a harsh or ugly word to each other, never heard either of them characterize each other in an ugly way. They set the tone. The final reason we came home was unconditional love. Mother and Dad always had a home of love. They loved each other and there was no question they loved us children."

The advantage of being a big family was that it was "love squared," George told me. That was part of the reason their family was strong—that, faith, and "some luck."

Texas, where that family was built, might have been another planet as George Bush talked that breezy summer day, gazing from time to time at the choppy sea beyond Walker's Point or fidgeting with a sundial on which Robert Browning's inscription invited: "Grow old along with me! The best is yet to be, the last of life, for which the first was made. Our times are in His hand."

From the tennis court nearby came the steady *thwack* of ball meeting racket. And meandering past, as directionless as Barbara's dog, were Bush grand-children in varying stages of need, whether of shoe-laces or Band-Aids or cookies. Puffy clouds skipped across the sky. Beyond Barbara's flower garden with the peonies she once planted to last a hundred years —"I'm planting for generations. I'm doing that for my children and grandchildren"—was a weathered cottage.

"We're close, we're very, very close," said George, thinking about those children and grandchildren and the family unit they formed. Then he motioned to-ward the cottage.

"The lady in that house makes us very, very close. My eighty-seven-year-old mother," he said. "She keeps it all together."

8

Friends, Neighbors, and Countrymen

"I am a good friend, a loyal friend. Now don't ask for an example."

*S*ometimes the two friends sat on the curb in front
of their mirror-image houses just catching up
with each other's life. Barbara's personality—
and in particular her energy—could be overwhelming, and some Washington political wives thought
being her neighbor might be taxing. But Shirley Pettis
Roberson, who lived next door for more than a
decade, didn't feel that way. "I never tried to keep
up," she said. "I went my way, did my thing, and
she went hers. We never encroached on one another."

They had known each other less than a year when
Barbara asked Shirley to run over with her one day
to look at a house she and George were thinking about

buying. Their husbands were freshmen members of the 90th Congress, and in the course of settling into Capitol Hill lives, the two women found they liked each other. Shirley started a legislative study group to which Barbara came that day, and afterward they drove to Palisade Lane to look at a pair of houses that were under construction. The Bushes had already decided on one, and seeing how much Shirley liked the other, Barabara suggested that she and her husband, Jerry, buy it.

The Bushes had moved to Washington, their fifteenth city in twenty-two years of marriage, after George won his race for Houston's new Seventh Congressional District seat. He had bought a house on Hillbrook Lane sight unseen from retiring Wyoming senator Milward Simpson in a deal worked out over the telephone. But there wasn't enough space or sunshine, and the plumbing didn't work right either, so the Bushes decided to move again, taking a loss on the house, which they liked to joke wasn't easy considering that real estate was to Washington what oil in those days was to Texas. Barbara found the twin brick houses being built on an out-of-the-way cul-de-sac that had all the elements the Bushes liked —children similar in ages to Doro, then seven; Marvin, ten; Neil, twelve; and Jeb, thirteen (George W. was twenty and at Yale); dogs; and interesting people, including Supreme Court associate justice Potter Stewart and his wife Mary Ann (Andy) and Franklin D. Roosevelt, Jr.

People living there had often wondered about

the vacant lot at the end of the street but had decided since it was so small nothing would ever be built there. Then, around 1967, to some dismay, the twin houses started going up, attractive enough but squashy, and people joked that, well, there went the neighborhood. "By golly," recalled Andy Stewart, who lived across the street, "in moved Bar and George." Within a short time, the Pettises followed. "And of course that was wonderful. Instead of being upset, we were blessed. They rapidly became astonishingly good neighbors."

In less than a week, Barbara had settled in and had her family's lives so organized that anyone who hadn't known otherwise would have supposed they had been there for years. She never procrastinated about anything that she put her mind to. "She'll get out in her garden and decide she has to weed from five in the morning to three in the afternoon, and she does," said Doro. Much as her mother might have decades earlier in Rye, Barbara took over a circular planted area at the end of the cul-de-sac as her project. Neighbors pitched in from time to time, but Barbara was the one who could be counted on to keep it mowed. She didn't always stop there. If Shirley and Jerry Pettis were home in their California district and the gardener they'd hired didn't mow their lawn as soon as Barbara thought he should have, she mowed it herself. "It happened any number of times—it infuriated me," said Shirley. "She didn't want the neighborhood going to pot. She always had good help inside and didn't particularly like that part of it, and she loved being in her garden. She would have wonderful, wonderful gardens. She would mulch them within an inch of their lives. So no one else's ever looked as nice as Bar's because she'd be out there with her shovel working in mulch."

The Bushes' backyard grill was going full blast almost immediately. "We were down there virtually every Sunday lunch," said Andy Stewart. "My husband never had a better time. They had this wonderful rapport with people, they made everybody feel at home. Everybody there was a new friend or someone from way back or somebody on the staff. And they always included their friends' children." Remembering back, Doro said, "My parents open their arms to people and make them feel part of the family. They really do have the most tremendous extended family of anybody I know. At Christmastime, when all of us were married, some of us came home, some couldn't. At the Christmas table would be the guy who's had a stroke, the guy who's just had a divorce, the person whose husband died, people who needed friends or family."

Barbara, who was very good on quantity cooking, did soup or chili ahead of time, and George took charge of the hamburgers over the outdoor grill, even in winter. Dessert was simple, ice cream on sticks most often, and service was help yourself. Talk, also plentiful, was about everything from sports and real estate to current events and politics, although on the latter Justice Stewart, who loved politics, always had to recuse himself. Part of what Andy and Potter Stewart found so enjoyable about the Bushes was their sense of humor. Barbara's was "killing." She had to watch herself in public, but at home, with people she could trust, she told stories as few others could, terribly funny ones in which she described her experiences, embellishing them with her flair for mimicry.

The Bushes quickly became a congressional couple to watch. George's thirty-nine other new Republican colleagues elected him president of the 90th Club, so named for that session of Congress. "It took all of three weeks before everybody decided George was destined for great stuff," said Janet Steiger, whose husband Bill was also a new congressman, from Wisconsin. George was being nurtured by more powerful Republicans, too, and thanks to them he had some fortunate breaks. Horse traders by nature, legislators ignored party lines in at least one instance: Democrat Wilbur Mills of Arkansas, chairman of the Ways and Means Committee, knew George's father from his Senate days, and when Prescott Bush asked him to help, Mills did what he could. George was assigned to Ways and Means, the first freshman congressman in either party to serve on that committee in sixty years.

Barbara made friends as quickly as George did. Janet Steiger met her at one of those large getacquainted activities arranged for congressional newcomers. "By the end of a couple of hours you knew there was a woman you wanted to know better. I think that was pretty much shared by everybody who met her. There was a sort of lively warmth, she seemed so real." Said Shirley Pettis Roberson, "I felt the fun of being with her immediately. I knew she had an excellent mind."

Wives of men in the 90th Club and in SOS, an invitation-only group of moderate Republicans with Yale and Harvard backgrounds, became part of Barbara's extended family. She not only remembered who they were, she remembered what they enjoyed. Art-history buffs were invited to go along to a National Gallery show. Flower nuts were urged to see a garden show with her. She gathered people to her —in airports, at the theater, or just walking down a street. They all joked about being another one of Barbara's 2,000 best friends. She tucked people into her activities, and she tucked herself into theirs. When Bill Steiger took Janet to the hospital for the birth of their son Billy, Janet remembered that "all of a sudden, this wonderful face was there checking on me. She'd worked her way into the labor room by announcing that she was my only relative in town."

Washington is full of men, egocentric and driven by political ambitions, who don't spend much time with their families. Barbara faced no more demands than other congressional wives doing the inevitable balancing act with children, husband, constituents, colleagues, and friends. George Bush may even have been better than most fathers, making it an office rule that his children's calls were priority and blocking out time for them on the weekends when he wasn't back in his congressional district. "But it all worked like silk for Barbara," said Janet Steiger. "I don't think the kids were out of touch, one with the other or they with their parents, for any period of time. There was tremendous bantering on some tremendous accomplishment, such as winning a tennis championship. They'd say, 'Yeah, but your backhand's weak.' They were never allowed to think they were anything above the norm. She was always there for them, she always knew where they were, she was endlessly picking them up. She never lost a focus on where her main concerns and responsibilities were, no matter what life changes occurred.

"Barbara improved on everything. You could invent something and she would make it better," said Janet, remembering a slide show she gave in Wisconsin. Barbara perfected it to the extent that she had a series of shows, one on the gardens of Washington, another on the buildings, and so on. "I ended up borrowing her slides. They were so much better," Janet said.

If she wasn't taking new pictures or making her children tour Washington ("My children have just gotten to like sight-seeing again," she joked in 1989), she was helping newly arrived Texas friends like Jessica Catto, whose husband was with the Organization of American States then, set up house by shopping for washing machines or bicycles. Once she even climbed through a window so Peggy Stanton, wife of another 90th Club member, could get into her own house; they had returned from a meeting to find the front door locked, the key inside rather than in Peggy's handbag.

"I am a good friend, a loyal friend. Now don't ask for an example," Barbara once said. When I asked her in 1989 what she looked for in a friend, she said, "I don't look for anything. I often find loyalty, humor, goodness. Hope they find the same from me."

They did. Once she became your friend, it seemed she was never far away when you needed her. When she and George learned that Jerry Pettis had been killed in a plane crash in 1975, they cabled Shirley from China, where George was chief of the U.S. Liaison Office, "Please come to us as soon as you can." In 1978 when Bill Steiger died of a massive heart attack, the Bushes immediately called Janet to say they were flying to Wisconsin. Bill had been the first to float George's name as a vice-presidential candidate at the GOP convention in 1968.

"I remember they arrived in a snowstorm," Janet said. "And after they went home, I had about ten days to decide whether to run for Bill's congressional seat. I was staring out the kitchen window and Bar called. She said, 'Here's what we're going to do. I made an appointment up at St. Alban's [a private Washington boys' school] and we're going to go up and talk and see what they think about Billy, academically and otherwise, whether he could take a semester off and go back to Wisconsin where he could live with his grandmother if you run.' It was an overwhelming kindness and it meant that when I made my decision, I made it as an informed decision. I just decided I was the only parent left and what was right for me was to be with Billy. But the point was that, once again, Bar gave me the tools to make the decision. She's done that so many times. Not to decide for me, but to let me know she was there to support whatever I decided to do."

"I don't think there are very many complicated relationships in her life," said George's sister, Nancy Ellis. "Her life isn't bogged down. She's never had to go talk over a relationship with a shrink. All her relationships are on an easy plane. She's sort of freed up to go and do wonderful things because she's not bottled up worrying about how does so-and-so feel about me or how do I feel about them. She's a tremendous help to his life—not an addition but a help."

George had only peripherally been involved in politics when he and Barbara lived in Midland during the 1950s. The joke was that in the precinct he chaired the Republicans received three votes on primary day—his, Barbara's, and that of a drunk who wandered in by mistake. The party wasn't in much better shape in Houston, where George moved his family —Barbara was pregnant with Doro—in 1959. He had amicably dissolved his partnership in Zapata Petroleum Corp., and with investor money arranged by his uncle Herbert, had bought its subsidiary offshore-drilling operation.

The Bushes were well off. They lived in the best neighborhood, belonged to the best country clubs, and their kids were in the best schools. George decided there was more out there to explore for than oil, a decision that surprised no one who knew George Bush. He was, after all, the son of a former U.S.

senator whom he idolized and against whom he had always judged himself, and his mother, whom he adored, had always told her children that they could do anything they put their minds to. Both had believed one ought to give something back to society for the advantages one enjoyed.

"Some people are motivated by money, some people by power, and some people by public service. I put George in that latter category," Barbara told me during that spring 1988 campaign swing in California. "He felt he'd made enough money for us to live and so he stopped working. He had no great ambitions to make a lot of money. I don't think you'd ever put George down as power mad. It's just public service."

By 1962, George's interest in politics had come to the attention of Harris County GOP leaders. John Tower's 1961 victory in the special election to fill Lyndon Johnson's U.S. Senate seat had offered hope to Texas Republicans after a hundred years as a virtual one-party state. Some thought they saw in George the catalyst they needed to bring warring conservative and moderate Republican factions together. So one Saturday morning a small group of Republican leaders visited him on Briar Drive to talk about the chairmanship of the county GOP. "When George told me, it never occurred to me that he had to *run* for office," said Barbara. Assuming the post was appointive, she took Doro, then three, to visit George's parents. She was in for a surprise when she returned.

There were 189 precincts in Harris County, and George and Barbara took his campaign into every one of them. Looking back twenty years later, with a half-dozen races behind them, Barbara called it the "hottest, meanest race" he ever ran. She was shocked to find hate literature under their door every morning. "That's pretty close," she complained.

George, who gave his speech about 189 times, joked that it was during that campaign that Barbara, on the platform listening, took up needlepoint so she wouldn't fall asleep. But she did more than needlepoint. Barbara was surprised to discover that she enjoyed campaigning. She always had good intuition about people and situations, but it began to develop into a political asset. She proved to be a quick learner. And George won the chairmanship.

Two years later, when he ran for the U.S. Senate, she wanted information, not flattery, on how her husband was doing. Her nametag read simply "Barbara," without the "Bush," when she and Jack Steele, one of the Harris County Republicans who had urged George to get into politics, made a door-to-door canvass of voters. "She was afraid if they knew who she was, they wouldn't give her an honest opinion of George."

Texas Republicans still didn't have their political act together, and one of the casualties was George Bush, who hadn't yet learned the art of the quick draw against a politician like incumbent Ralph Yarborough, a liberal Lyndon Johnson ally. Even Barbara's father, Marvin Pierce, by then the president of the McCall Corporation, became an issue when the John Birch Society circulated literature suggesting that *Redbook* magazine, which McCall's published, was an official Communist Party organ. When Yarborough likened Bush to ultraconservative Barry Goldwater, charging that he did not care that nuclear bombs "would create leukemia and cancer in babies," Martin Allday, George's campaign manager, got "mad as heck." Allday knew that George had set up the Bright Star Foundation for leukemia research after Robin's death, and he advised him to tell voters about Robin. A few hours before the final television campaign pitch, the two were at a health club talking about what George could say to stem the Yarborough tide. "I said, 'It seems to me you could turn that accusation about leukemia around and use it to your advantage,' " Allday said. Replied George, "I'm not going to bring that up."

George's defeat—43.6 percent to Yarborough's 56.2—hit five-year-old Doro Bush hard. When she saw a sobbing Don Rhodes, a campaign aide who was like a member of the family, "I remember not really understanding what happened but getting into the car and being in tears. My dad turned to me and said, 'Doro, what's wrong with you?' He knew, obviously, that I wasn't upset because he had lost. And I said, 'Dad, I'll be the only one in school who has a father without a job.' " George, who would sell his Zapata Off-Shore stock for $1 million and get out of the oil business soon after, said, " 'Doro, don't worry about that. We'll be fine.' "

There was some benefit to be derived from the Senate defeat: George at least had achieved name recognition. Less than two years later George ran for the U.S. House, becoming the first Republican to win a seat from Harris County. His entry into congressional politics was seen by some, including his boyhood friend FitzGerald Bemiss, as only the beginning. Bemiss remembered that his own father wrote Prescott Bush then to say that if George used his many assets correctly, he would probably be president of the United States someday. Certainly by 1968 his political star seemed to be ascendant. "He didn't have an opponent and I remember saying to Bar, if I didn't love you so much, I'd hate you for the ease of your second campaign," said Shirley Pettis Roberson.

Barbara was turning into the consummate political wife who seldom forgot a name, the face that went with it, or any of the details connected with the first meeting. But she was shy about public speaking. Shirley remembered that Barbara came to her one day on Palisade Lane saying that she was supposed to address a garden club in the home district, and there was no way she could do it. " 'Listen, Bar, anybody who can be scintillating at their dinner or luncheon table and always be the center of all the sparkle can give a speech. You'll be great,' " Shirley said. "Our studies were across from each other on the third floor of these four-story houses, and I would see her light and know she was slaving over a speech. She wouldn't admit how much time she put into it."

"She always knew what she believed in and she had always been able to meet and talk to people, but in the beginning she never thought of making speeches," said Mildred Kerr, who became Barbara's friend when the Bushes moved to Houston. Marion Chambers lived there by then, too, and Barbara arrived on her doorstep to say she had come to practice. "She stood in front of the fireplace and we both started laughing because we could hear her knees knocking," Marion said. "That was the last time I ever heard them knock." Said Barbara years later of her shyness, "For someone who has an open mouth on every subject now, it seems amazing."

In some ways, she was better before an audience than George. "When she talks to an audience there is straight projection. The audience feels this is a real person. She is able to assert strength, ideas, and feelings of personal warmth without trying. George Bush is as genuine as you can get, but Barbara Bush is a direct link with her audience. You don't get the idea you are listening to an appendage [to Bush]," said Victor Gold, a senior campaign aide and coauthor of George's autobiography.

By 1969, President Richard Nixon was urging George to make another try for the U.S. Senate. Prescott Bush was unconvinced, particularly since George's congressional seat had been uncontested in his reelection campaign. Barbara cast George's decision in a different light. "He loved the Congress, but I suspect he found it very frustrating. It moves slowly and sometimes not at all. A congressman has about 450,000 constituents, all of whom think you are as close as your telephone. I'll never forget the night our phone rang at four A.M. and a fuzzy voice said, 'Sorry to call you at this hour, George, but I thought this was a good time to catch you at home.' "

George hadn't expected Yarborough, the incumbent, to be beaten in the primary by Lloyd Bentsen, Jr., who like George was a World War II pilot with strong conservative ties in the Houston business community. Against Yarborough the lines would have been sharply drawn; against Bentsen the race was an entirely different battle. George leaned heavily on his White House connections; besides a campaign appearance by Nixon, help came in the form of about $100,000 from a fund Nixon kept for his preferred candidates. Barbara worked hard in that campaign, too, and when George lost, 53.4 percent to 46.6 percent, she took it hard. "Losing is very painful," she acknowledged. "Maybe more painful for the wife than the husband." "When I called her up after the loss of the Senate election, she couldn't stop crying," Nancy Ellis remembered years later.

But once Nixon knew what George wanted to do, he was ready to help again. "The next thing we knew we were in New York City, where George was the permanent representative to the United Nations. . . . It was like being taken around the world to meet people from a hundred twenty-eight countries, and yet never having to pack a bag or sleep in a strange bed," Barbara told her American University audience in 1985.

There were political difficulties. For one thing, George had avoided foreign policy issues in Congress—"He was on the Ways and Means Committee and we had to keep our priorities. It would have been luxury," Barbara told an interviewer in his defense —so his nomination had triggered some demurrals. With guidance from Nixon, George proved to be an able enough student of foreign affairs; the problems came with the positions. He dutifully tried to justify U.S. involvement in Vietnam, a no-win proposition, and he championed Taiwan's UN membership. Six months into his job he was surprised to read one day that Henry Kissinger, Nixon's national security adviser, had made a secret visit to Beijing. It was a trip that paved the way for Nixon's historic visit the following winter, but it also marked a more immediate turning point in relations with the People's Republic of China. George quickly espoused America's new two-Chinas position—another losing proposition, since the UN voted to expel Taiwan when it admitted the People's Republic.

In the rather formal official ambassador's residence at the Waldorf Towers, Barbara proclaimed Bush family pride in America by showing off only the work of U.S. artists, serving local wines, and buying only American-made clothing. She loved the life. Now she took her needlepoint to Security Council debates. "You try not to sit with someone your husband's going to vote against," she told an interviewer. "But if it happens, nobody bats an eyelash. They're a very sophisticated crowd." The Bushes entertained that crowd at receptions and dinners in their Waldorf Towers apartment, took them to Connecticut for Bush family picnics, invited them to baseball games of the New York Mets, among whose owners was George's uncle Herbert, and introduced them to their powerful Washington friends. "They loved to share," said Shirley Pettis Roberson. "It was an integral part of the Bush phenomena. At the United Nations during a particularly challenging or exciting debate, they didn't want to have it all to themselves, so they would invite us up for a dinner. . . . If somebody was uncomfortable, she'd right away ease the situation."

Socially, the Bushes were a smashing success during their twenty-two months in New York. "I'd pay to have this job," Barbara said.

But early in 1973, with the Watergate scandal simmering but not yet at a rolling boil, Nixon asked George to be chairman of the Republican National Committee. Barbara was less than enchanted; she knew some of their friends felt it was a "dead end" for a politician. But George, one of Nixon's loyal supporters, couldn't say no to the President, and the Bushes moved back to Washington. As new revelations incriminated Nixon, George was handed damage control. "It was like a leaky roof, where you're running around with pots trying to stop the water," Barbara said. "George used to say it was like being married to a centipede, and it kept dropping shoes."

In the middle of it all, in October 1973, Vice President Spiro Agnew resigned because of a scandal about kickbacks and systematic payoffs while he was governor of Maryland. Nixon named Gerald Ford, then the House minority leader, his vice president. In summer 1974, when the Supreme Court forced Nixon to surrender tape recordings that left no doubt he had tried to obstruct justice, George Bush who had staunchly defended Nixon up until then, assessed the effect. He wrote Nixon on August 7: "It is my considered judgment that you should now resign." George's voice was only one of many in the GOP. The next day Nixon stepped down. "This was very naive, I realize, but Nixon really fooled us," said Barbara.

The Bushes retreated to Kennebunkport, hopeful that Ford would reward George for his loyalty to the party by naming him vice president. But no such luck, despite George's popularity within the GOP. In one of Ford's polls of GOP leaders, Bush led with 125 votes to Nelson Rockefeller's 100 in a field of eleven names. George was more than disappointed when Rockefeller got the nod; he was angry. He wanted out as RNC chairman, and as consolation, the Ford White House offered him an ambassadorship. There was talk of London or Paris, but George wanted to try something different: The People's Republic of China. By October he was in Beijing heading the 226-member staff at the U.S Liaison Office.

It was Barbara's first trip abroad, and she described it later as "a whole new leaf in both our lives. We studied together and shared everything." "China was wonderful," Barbara told Marty Primeau of the *Dallas Morning News* a decade later. "Watergate was a terrible experience, so to go off to China and learn a whole new culture was beautiful. I loved the people. I loved the whole feeling."

She also loved being with George, together without interruptions for the first time in years. The children were at schools back in the States. Barbara went home to see them for Christmas, while George's mother and aunt joined him in China. There were other visitors, nonstop, including Henry Kissinger and Gerald Ford. George and Barbara kept up their tennis, though China was where they gave up playing doubles together. Describing the decision to George Plimpton, Barbara said they were playing a Pakistani, a man who wasn't very good, and an East German woman, who was. Barbara thought the woman must have been taking steroids because there had to be some reason she and her partner were trouncing the Bushes. "In any event, I clutched, and George was so disappointed, especially to be beaten by the East German, that afterward I told him I knew he preferred men's doubles and that was perfectly all right with me."

By December 1975, the Bushes were back in Washington. Ford had asked George to come home to head the controversial Central Intelligence Agency in a shakeup of administration jobs. George saw the appointment as effectively removing him from consideration as Ford's running mate in 1976. Barbara was no more enthusiastic about his taking the post than she had been about his heading the RNC in 1973. She was also concerned about how the new job would affect the lives of their children. Having a father who was head of the RNC during Watergate had been difficult for them in their peer groups. "We talked to our oldest boy and said, 'Now you check around and find out how the others feel,' " she said. "They were all at a sensitive age, college and high school age, and he checked, thought it over, and said, 'Take the job and come home. We want you home.' "

But the prospect of George on the hot seat again was obviously on Barbara's mind when, shortly after the announcement, she wrote a letter to a friend, saying, "I shall curl up every time I read or hear a mean word about George, and he tells me that in this new job I'll see and hear one heck of a lot!"

Back in their old Palisade Lane neighborhood life necessarily changed. The place swarmed with secret agents. Every license plate was recorded and every arrival and departure noted. Shirley Pettis Roberson, who had been elected to her late husband's congressional seat, had started to date again. She teased George that twenty-four-hour surveillance was a dastardly thing to do to her. "If he knew there was someone who wasn't a particular favorite of mine, he'd drop a little note in the mailbox: 'If you need any help getting rid of this guy, just call.' "

He signed it "Head Spook."

Barbara, knowing she and George wouldn't be able to "share" as much, said later it was her "least favorite" of the jobs George held. After George became vice president she "edited slightly" a book to raise money for literacy, *C. Fred's Story: A Dog's Life*. In it, C. Fred wrote that he and Barbara knew absolutely nothing about George's job. "He said Bar and I couldn't keep a secret, therefore he didn't tell us anything. He was right about Bar. Her favorite sentence starts with, 'Don't tell George I told you, but . . .' He was wrong about me . . ."

9

Cause for Concern

"I once spent the summer thinking of all the things that bothered me—teen pregnancy, drugs, everything—and I realized everything would be better if more people could read and write."

There was a point after the children were gone when the feminist movement was gathering momentum that Barbara began to have some doubts about what she'd done with her life. She went through a difficult time, uneasy about her homemaker role, feeling like "I'm sitting home—just sitting home." For the first time in her married life there were no babies, no Little League games, no car pools, no meetings with teachers, no political campaigns, no diplomatic roles—no projects of any consequence needed her.

It was the midseventies, a time when the traditional roles of housewife and mother were caught in a tug of war between the most extreme feminists and the conservative women's backlash the movement had created, and Barbara Bush, a reflective woman who intimates said usually had no dark sides, was at a personal crossroads.

It was also a time when the Republican Party, after forty years of supporting the Equal Rights Amendment, was under increasing pressure from within to withdraw its endorsement. That would come in 1980 when the ultraconservative wing of the party succeeded in dropping the proposed amendment from the convention platform. In accepting second spot on the ticket that Ronald Reagan headed that year, George Bush abandoned his earlier support for ERA, and Barbara stepped back from hers as well. Two years later the ERA fell three states short of the thirty-eight it needed to become the twenty-seventh amendment to the U.S. Constitution.

"I don't think it was too hard," James Baker III, Bush's campaign chairman that year, said of George's decision to give up on ERA. "When you go on the ticket as vice president, your job is to support the president. You're not supposed to advocate independent positions."

"The amendment was given a fair shot at approval and failed. . . . Both Reagan and I believed that the best way to secure equal rights for women is through legislation, not constitutional amendment," George wrote in *Looking Forward* in 1987.

Though they didn't succeed in getting it back on the platform, Republican moderates continued to lobby for reinstatement of the ERA in 1988, arguing, as Rep. Bill Green of New York did before a GOP platform committee meeting in Washington March 30, that "the underlying issue of equality for women remains active and popular." Citing a study for the Hearst Corporation, Green described the essence of that issue this way: "While some arch-conservatives view the working woman as nontraditional, history shows that the stereotype of a woman only leaving her parents' home to get married and have children is based not upon a long history but upon one atypical generation: the post-WWII experience. Today's woman, electing for education equal to that of men, substantial work experience, delayed marriage, and both delayed and limited childbearing, reflects her grandmother and great-grandmother's experience and desires."

George, at the head of the ticket by then, did not rejoin the support for ERA, and neither did Barbara. "There we go, asking that question," she chided the group of reporters at the Vice President's House in January 1989. "I want equal rights for women, men, everybody. Equal rights for every American. Equal pay for equal work." Did that mean she could support an amendment? "No. I'm not against it or for it. I'm not talking about it."

Barbara belonged to that "atypical generation" of women who after World War II opted to raise families and stay home rather than get into the work force and stay there. Though she had dropped out of college as a sophomore, she always knew she could have gone back had she wanted. "George would have been more than willing. I might have had to wait a little bit, but he would have worked it out," she told me in Califorina. She could have gotten a job, too, but as the wife and daughter of successful business-men, she had never had to go to work because of financial need. "You know, I've been allowed an enormous luxury, which was I didn't have to work for money," she said after she was in the White House. "But I wouldn't have minded it if I'd had to."

Despite all that, the women's movement and the empty-nest syndrome had combined to shake her complacency in the mid-1970s. "I have to confess that at a certain point in our life when our children were all gone, I went through sort of a—well, sort of a difficult time really because suddenly women's lib had made me feel that my life had been wasted," she said in 1989. But that didn't last long, only about six months, she said. She credited George with making her realize how wrong she was, how working two or three days a week as a nursing-home volunteer, doing a lot of luncheon speaking, and entertaining were important, too.

She had always been active but never more so than with the hectic schedule she kept during the eight years she was Second Lady. She hosted 1,192 events at the Vice President's House and attended 1,232 Washington events outside the residence—an average of six per week, more than half of which were for the Republican Party. In 1985 when someone wrote asking if besides playing tennis and doing needlepoint

Barbara and George take an impromptu nap aboard Air Force Two, on the 1984 campaign trail just two weeks before the Reagan/Bush team was reelected to a second term. (*David Valdez/The White House*)

At the Vice President's House after a doubles match on October 7, 1987, featuring George Bush and Crown Prince Akihito of Japan. The athletes cool down with Barbara. (*David Valdez/The White House*)

Barbara in her element, gardening at Kennebunkport, August 6, 1988. She loves to mix wildflowers with garden flowers. She has a particular fondness for peonies, lilies, gardenias, and all varieties of daisies. She is known to spend hours on end in her garden, which she considers a sort of therapy. (*David Valdez/The White House*)

Barbara and George enjoying a moment together in their Kennebunkport garden. Criticized during the 1988 campaign for not publicly demonstrating their affection for each other, Barbara said, "He and I are very affectionate in our own way. We are the most happily married couple. We don't have to pretend for people." (*David Valdez/The White House*)

In addition to her family, friends, and gardening, the First Lady's passions include dogs. She admires one of Millie's new puppies. (*Carol T. Powers/The White House*)

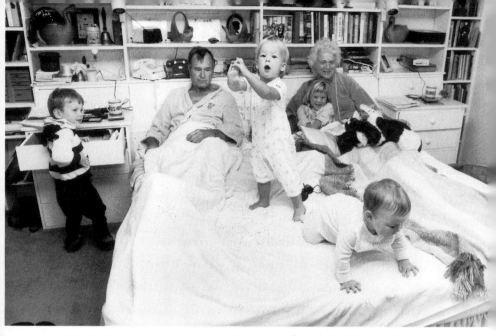

The Bushes' bedroom becomes a playground for grandchildren at Kennebunkport. August 22, 1987. (*David Valdez/The White House*)

Grandma is the center of attention during storytime at Kennebunkport. Her literacy campaign begins at home. August 7, 1988. (*David Valdez/The White House*)

Barbara fixes lunch while son Neil looks on. Lunches at Kennebunkport are usually simple and relaxed. (*David Valdez/The White House*)

George's mother, Dorothy Walker Bush, is the family matriarch and has a home in the Bushes' Walker Point compound near the main house. Four generations of Bushes together here in Kennebunkport. *Left to right*: Dorothy Walker Bush, George, Barbara, and Dorothy ("Doro") Bush LeBlond with her daughter Ellie. (*David Valdez/The White House*)

For Barbara Bush, caring comes in a variety of ways. In Frankfurt, she and George greet released hostages of hijacked TWA Flight 847 on July 1, 1985. (*David Valdez/The White House*)

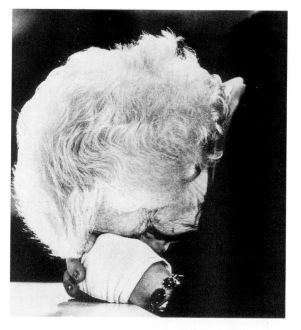

Barbara mourns during a memorial service for slain Swedish Prime Minister Olaf Palme at Washington's National Presbyterian Church on March 7, 1986. (*Dayna Smith/* Washington Post)

The proud grandparents with Marshall Bush at her christening, June 17, 1986.
(*David Valdez/The White House*)

The Bush family cheers as George goes over the top in the delegate count.
New Orleans, Republican National Convention, August 17, 1988. (*David Valdez/The White House*)

The new President works in the Oval Office while the First Lady studies the photographs. Millie roams about, exploring her new home. January 27, 1989. (*Susan Biddle/The White House*)

she ate bonbons, she sent back a similar numerical accounting of her activities, and finished with a little campaign plug for George. "If you think my schedule is full, George Bush's makes me look like all I do is sit home, do needlepoint, play tennis, and eat bonbons," she quipped. Then, summing up her philosophy of life, she added, "I have always felt that one had two choices: you can either like what you do or you can dislike it. I have chosen to like it."

Nonetheless, she was defensive about her "traditional" image during the 1988 campaign. Even after she was in the White House she seemed still hurt by a question NBC's *Today* host Jane Pauley had asked in the course of an interview in 1988. Pauley said, "Mrs. Bush, people say George is a man for the eighties and you're a woman of the forties," and asked, "What do you say to that?" As Barbara remembered it, "I said, 'If you mean I love my family, my country, and my God, so be it,' but I felt like crying."

She certainly had never thought of herself as an anachronism. She didn't believe that her generation had opted out, that the practice of staying home and rearing the children had been a generational pattern. "No, no, absolutely not. I think many women [now] are making an enormous sacrifice—I'm talking financially—in staying home. But the rewards are great. I think a lot of new books have come out now talking about how important mothers are," she said in the March 1989 session with journalists. She knew she was not alone in her opinion that "women's lib has made it very hard for some women to stay home," and she came to the defense of women like herself who had done it. It certainly wasn't because they couldn't do anything else, she said. "I think many women, certainly of my generation, can run the world. And some of them have waited until their children have gone off and they've been grandparents and have taken on major projects for money."

Barbara hadn't been around working women with children much when she became Second Lady and got an office and a staff of her own, and she was skeptical of women who continued to work after they had babies. "She didn't imply that I shouldn't do it," said Susan Porter Rose, Barbara's chief of staff and mother of one. But her sentiment was discernible, Rose said. "Women are home with their babies. Period. And that's how you're a mother. And you're not a good mother if you don't do that. But I think our little office and our little staff that had three who were mothers, I think seeing that work was enlightening for her."

By the time she entered the White House, half of all American women worked outside the home, according to a Ford Foundation study. More than half of all mothers with school age children had jobs, according to the census bureau. A Hudson Institute report predicted that by the year 2000, 60 percent of entrants into the work force would be women, and reported that polls showed teenage women expected not only to have careers throughout adulthood but also to be married and have children.

Barbara said she respected women who had made

that choice—"I'm not critical. I have daughters [-in-law] who work. I don't think it's easy"—but she also had a strong belief that neither men nor women can truly have it all. As she told Enid Nemy of the *New York Times* in 1984, "I don't think men and women should have children and not take the responsibility. Men are going to have to take a lot more responsibility. They will have to do more as their share. But women are also going to have to learn that they have to have priorities, that they have to make choices, and that they can't have everything. You can't, in my opinion, be a bank president and a full-time mother."

In the final analysis, Barbara saw a clear difference—"absolutely," she told me—between women who chose to work and women who had to work, and it was the latter she was concerned about. "Those are the people I'm trying to help with my literacy and education projects and my interest in it. Those are the people, not the people who choose to work, although some of those obviously need help, too, but they don't come under this category of people we're interested in helping."

People close to the Bushes described Barbara as "genuinely interested" in helping people, and George as "genuinely interested" in serving the nation—and helping people in that way. If the emphasis differed, they saw it as a matter of "practical politics" on his part.

Barbara was practical about her politics, too, though in a different way; she concentrated on what she could accomplish—without causing political problems—and tried not to worry about what she couldn't. When I asked her once how it felt to believe in something that she knew was not politically expedient, she said, "Let me tell you, I put an emphasis on things I'm interested in. . . . I try to keep my focus. I want to make a difference, and I might just as well do it by focusing on the things I'm interested in. . . . I'm interested in literacy and homelessness and AIDS, things that really aren't very controversial but need taking care of. . . . Why should I worry about those things which are political? I mean, everything has a side. Half the people are going to hate you anyway."

It was a political reality she knew well. Jimmy Carter hadn't been president very long in 1977 when George Bush began to give serious thought to running for the job himself. He had friends all around the country from his days as RNC chairman, a grassroots network he felt he could build upon much as Carter had done with the Democrats. After a trip to the People's Republic of China that fall, he and Jim Baker, who had managed Gerald Ford's 1976 presidential campaign, returned to Houston to set up The Fund for Limited Government.

The following summer, at George's invitation, domestic and foreign policy experts from within the Republican Party went to Kennebunkport to help him assess his prospects. When she was not arranging clambakes or lobster feeds and finding beds for everybody, Barbara was sitting in on the briefing sessions at the rectory of St. Ann's Church, where Bushes and

Walkers had worshiped for decades. After those meetings, as she jogged, she assimilated what she had heard. "I once spent the summer thinking of all the things that bothered me—teen pregnancy, drugs, everything—and I realized everything would be better if more people could read and write," she said later of those weeks in Kennebunkport.

In the fall of 1978, George returned to Kennebunkport to continue his meetings. Barbara returned to China with her sister-in-law. "She went back to brush up on her slides because I think she had a feeling that she was going to use them in 1980 as an entrée in speaking to people about her husband," said Nancy Ellis.

Fired by the excitement of being back in a country whose culture and people had fascinated her, she was an impressive tour guide. Staying with American friends assigned to the U.S. Liaison Mission, she and Nancy Ellis put on their blue jeans and sneakers and rode bicycles around Beijing, visiting historic sites Barbara had come to know three years earlier. Nancy Ellis said later she never felt that Barbara was deciding anything in particular, just crystallizing her impressions of a place that had added such a dimension to her life. The two of them had a number of discussions, but one in particular struck Nancy Ellis because of the certainty in Barbara's voice.

"She said to me one morning—she told me later she'd forgotten this—'Well, you know your brother's going to be president of the United States, don't you?' 'My God,' I said, 'what are you talking about?' She said, 'Well, he is. He is. I can just see it coming.' And she said it in a way that was just a fait accompli," said Nancy Ellis.

By the time George announced his candidacy in May 1979, Barbara realized she, too, was ready for something more. She thought of herself as a "late bloomer," she told me in 1988. "I believe in passages, times in your life. I think there was a time in my life where I really nested and was a mother. And then, I mean, I went to China and really delved deeply into it, into the history. I really think it's good for you to get a new subject about every ten years. Unless you have a burning desire to be a doctor or a president of a bank, probably it's a good thing to shift jobs, meet new people, take on new projects."

Few First Ladies ever left the White House without being identified with some project. As the symbol of what the American woman should be, the president's wife, by the late nineteenth century, was looked to as someone of virtue and reliability who took an interest in matters within the woman's sphere of home and family. Of high rank or birth, she felt an obligation to be generous and responsible for her time and attention, whether directed toward church work, an orphanage, or those with physical afflictions. Eleanor Roosevelt, who in the eyes of her critics took the idea to the extreme with her involvement in civil rights and other humanitarian causes, became the role model for those who followed. By the 1960s, women whose husbands wanted to be president knew they had to have a cause. The more successful expanded their personal interests: Jacqueline Kennedy's in historic preservation, Lady Bird Johnson's in the environment, Betty Ford's in women's rights. Others, such as Rosalynn Carter with mental health and Nancy Reagan with drug abuse, developed their causes from their husbands' days as governors. Barbara Bush belonged to both groups.

She had a lifelong interest in volunteer work; through the years, she had always done some sort—at Yale, raising money for the United Negro College Fund; in Midland, starting the thrift shop for a service league after Robin died; in Houston, Washington, and New York, volunteering in nursing homes and hospitals. In New York, while George was Nixon's ambassador to the United Nations, Barbara had volunteered at Sloan-Kettering, where in 1953 she had spent so many months with Robin.

But she wanted to go beyond that. As a 1985 *Los Angeles Times* story quoted her, "By the time my George had decided to run for high office, I decided that I should find a cause." In her speech at American University she said she had wanted to do "something that would not be controversial, [that would] help the most people possible and maybe not cost more government money." She even invoked Lady Bird Johnson: "It would be sad to pass up a bully pulpit. It's a fleeting chance to do something for your country that makes your heart sing." And as Lady Bird also said, "If your project is useful and people notice it, and that reflects well on your husband, heavens, that's one of your biggest roles in life."

Barbara went about finding her cause the same way she approached everything in her life—through meticulous self-organization. "I think there was a keen realization that if you made that run for president, you were looking at two years of very vigorous efforts on the parts of both Bar and George. Given the limits of time, she started to sort out what she wanted to concentrate on," remembered Janet Steiger, whose husband Bill, a congressman from Wisconsin, was among those Republicans George had consulted. "She began to see the connections the inability to read had with crime rates, juvenile delinquency, world peace, teenage pregnancies, and unemployment, and that illiteracy echoed through the whole fabric of society."

She had come from a family of "omnivorous readers." And ever since Neil Bush's teachers had gently but firmly warned Barbara and George that their son's dyslexia might prevent him from going on to college, she had been interested in how reading problems affected the quality of one's life. With her usual matter-of-fact approach, she had attacked Neil's disability by arranging for tutors and extensive testing, helping him with practice tapes, finding books with large print, and never giving up. "Reading disability isn't a class thing, it isn't racial, it happens to anybody. Unless a parent is supportive, well-prepared, and recognizes the problem, a child can be lost forever. And my mother was very stubborn about it, lining up specialists, making sure I saw them," said Neil, who never minded looking at the sports pages.

"She was clear-minded and had all the confidence in the world that I would be a success, and she got me through it." Her efforts were rewarded when Neil not only earned a bachelor's degree from Tulane University in 1977, but also was awarded his master's degree two years later.

By January 1980, George's two years on the stump seemed to be paying off. He came out of the Iowa caucuses with a 31 percent to 29 percent margin over Ronald Reagan, and there were wins in five other primaries.

Barbara, too, was drawing some attention. In media interviews, she said that as First Lady she would concentrate her energies on literacy and volunteerism, working for organizations such as Reading Is Fundamental, the country's largest reading motivation program, which she first learned about when she heard a speech by its founder, Margaret McNamara, wife of John F. Kennedy's secretary of defense. Reading of Barbara's interest, Mrs. McNamara and RIF president Ruth Graves invited her to join their board—whatever the outcome of George Bush's campaign. She promptly accepted. "She was a great force in helping unite the literacy groups," said Janet Steiger. "Always quietly, never with any big show."

In May, George's "Big Mo," as he had tagged his earlier momentum, had started to fizzle. Ronald Reagan won the primary in George's home state of Texas. Jim Baker decided it was time to tell George he had better pull out. Their meeting lasted all day because George said he didn't want to be a quitter and abandon people working for him in states where primaries were still ahead. Publicly, Barbara was on his side. "Hang in There George" read the limited-edition campaign button she wore when she served sandwiches and coffee to reporters staking out her front lawn. But by evening, George withdrew from the race.

Two months later when the Republican National Convention opened in Detroit, the big question of who Ronald Reagan's running mate would be seemed to have been answered. A dispirited group of Bush supporters watched television in George and Barbara's suite at the Pontchartrain Hotel, expecting the announcement that Gerald Ford had been chosen. Then the telephone rang. It was Ronald Reagan. Greenwich friend Betsy Heminway remembered being shooed out of the room by Barbara, then having to go back because she had forgotten her handbag. "Pretend you haven't heard this," Barbara whispered, explaining that Reagan had just asked George to be his running mate.

The Bushes settled into the Vice President's House in January 1981, and Barbara went to work keeping her own campaign promise to fight illiteracy. She knew that an estimated 23 million adult Americans were functionally illiterate, lacking basic skills beyond the fourth-grade level, and that the reading and writing skills of another 30 to 35 million did not go beyond the eighth-grade level. "They can't read signs in a department store. They don't know what the directions on a medicine bottle say. They can't

look in the want ads for a job or fill out a job appli-
cation form," she wrote in an op-ed essay in the *Washington Post* in 1984. "The personal cost to these people
is very high. They suffer the frustration of constant
helplessness and the continuing fear of being found
out and humiliated."

She was a tireless volunteer for her cause; in eight
years as the vice president's wife, she attended 537
events related to literacy and 129 to volunteerism at
schools, prisons, factories, learning centers, and any-
place else that needed her name and presence to advance those causes. In 1983, she split $40,000 in
royalties from her book, *C. Fred's Story*, between two
groups, Laubach Literacy Action and Literacy Volunteers of America. She was the inspiration for cre-
ation of the Business Council for Effective Literacy,
set up by Harold W. McGraw, Jr., chief executive
officer of the publishing firm of McGraw-Hill. In
1985, she endorsed a joint public service undertaking
by Capital Cities/ABC and the Public Broadcasting
Service called Project Literacy U.S. (PLUS), a massive campaign to heighten awareness of illiteracy and
motivate people into action through on-air program-
ming and community task forces. "She's more than
a cheerleader. She's somebody who helps and sup-
ports efforts that already exist and moves them to the
next plateau so they all work together," said Margot
Woodwell, PBS PLUS project director.

Behind the scenes of George's 1988 presidential
campaign Susan Porter Rose, assisted by others in
the literacy movement, had been planning a mid-

November tribute to Barbara for her work on behalf of literacy—whatever the outcome of the election. Also in the works was a foundation to fight illiteracy. About a week before the election, Susan told Barbara what was going on. "I said, 'It's a wrap-up if we lose, it's a launch if we win, so it doesn't matter if [the Vice President] wins or loses.' She said, 'But what if he has something to do?' And I said, 'Mrs. Bush, this has been on the Vice President's schedule for a year and a half.'"

Within two months after she became First Lady, Barbara announced plans for the Barbara Bush Foundation for Family Literacy, with a pledged starter fund of $1 million in corporate, foundation, and individual donations to be used on what she called "intergenerational activities." "We all know that adults with reading problems tend to raise children with reading problems," she said in announcing the foundation at a White House luncheon. "And when I talk about family literacy, I am talking about families of all kinds: the big and bouncing kind, the single parent, extended families, divorced, homeless, and migrant." She saw the family as the nucleus for literacy as "a universal value in the nation."

Also behind the scenes, there was increasing political evidence that Barbara was more than just the candidate's wife doing some surrogate speaking. Aides described her as George's "social conscience," making unpublicized visits to homeless shelters so she could hear for herself the circumstances that had put people there.

"We've got to acknowledge the fact—and do something about—thirty percent of our homeless who are women with children," she told me during the May 1988 campaign swing in California. "Men are not being made accountable for the children. That is something George has campaigned on, and it is absolutely outrageous. We've collected enormous amounts of money and it's just a drop in the hat for what's being owed to those children. It's terrible and I don't know how people face themselves. They go on and have new families and don't help the women. The children I worry about, really, the teenage pregnancies. These people need help."

Her empathy with people in less fortunate circumstances had contributed to her work with groups dedicated to wiping out illiteracy. "You have to show caring," she said. Both she and George had worked hard for the communities in which they lived, but unlike George, whom some saw as very much a captive of his privileged upbringing and his early career goals, Barbara had broadened her experience through her own natural curiosity, interests, and experiences. Some had changed her life. Once, in 1957, when she was driving between Kennebunkport and Midland with the children, she met head-on the ugliness of bigotry. Little Rock, scene of crisis in school integration, had erupted in August, and as she and Otha Fitzgerald Taylor, a black woman helping with the children, were driving through the South, they found they couldn't eat in the same restaurants. Otha wanted her to feed the babies in the restaurant and get a room and said she'd stay in the car. "But I made up my mind that we were a team," said Barbara. So they all ate and slept together in the same room. "Of course it made a difference. It made us less tolerant of bigotry," she said. "And I discovered I was more stubborn than I thought."

While her "major" cause was literacy, she said in 1989, she was also taking on AIDS and the homeless because they were "sort of education things, I believe a lot of that is—certainly in AIDS, a lot of it is education." She believed that "if more people could read, we'd have less problems. We'd have less teenage pregnancies, we would have less unwanted babies . . . that's my new answer for every question because it's true," she said in the American University speech.

In the 1988 campaign George was supporting adoption as a solution to those unwanted pregnancies, opposing abortion except in cases of rape, incest, or when the mother's life was at stake. Adoption was a solution especially dear to the Bushes' hearts. Son Marvin and his wife, Margaret, had adopted a daughter in 1986. "My view on adoption has certainly been altered somewhat," Marvin told me in August 1988. "I think what a horrible crime it would have been for Marshall's mom to abort when I see this miracle I live with."

Barbara, who had "planned" all of her children, was evasive when the abortion issue came up. In Houston where she was once thought to have been involved with Planned Parenthood—though there was no record of that—members of that group's board asked her help in "cooling the rhetoric" that led to a series of clinic bombings in the mideighties. "We got a nice handwritten note back to the effect that she had friends on both sides of the issue and that she felt like the man from Kentucky during the Civil War, with a blue shirt and gray pants. She said the abortion issue was vexing to her from a personal point of view and that the number of abortions especially pained her knowing that her son was struggling to adopt a baby. She was taking a very thoughtful but neutral position and was judicious in the use of her endorsement of anything," said Peter Durkin, executive director of Houston Planned Parenthood.

Clearly, the situation wasn't simple to her, and in March 1989 when asked by reporters if she thought the Supreme Court should overturn *Roe v. Wade*, the landmark 1973 decision giving women the right to choose abortion, she seemed uncomfortable, and uncharacteristically inarticulate. "Now, listen," she told them, "you can try this every way you know—I am not going to discuss that. But that really—first of all, I don't think it's very presidential. I don't think it's —it's not—I don't think it's—I'm not going to talk about it. I'm not—because, see, if I start talking about one issue, then I have to move into another and another and another."

Had her husband asked her views on the issue? "I don't think he asked me." And had she made her views known to him? "Many, many years ago—I mean, many, many years ago . . . If I told you the response or reaction, you'd know what he and I were—" Then, having broken off in midsentence, she said, laughing, "Keep trying."

On April 9, 1989, as the Supreme Court was about to hear arguments in a case some feared could reverse the 1973 decision, crowds that were variously estimated at 300,000 to 600,000 turned out at the U.S. Capitol for a rally urging the court to preserve freedom of choice. One huge sign reading "Barbara Bush Is Pro-Choice" was visible from the White House as the procession passed along Constitution Avenue. Later, Barbara kindled hopes of impassioned marchers by saying, "That's what America is all about and it's great." With George Bush in favor of reversing prochoice abortion laws, Barbara's office issued a clarification: She was referring to the right of any group to protest. She was not backing the prochoice movement.

Media interpretation had been "misconstrued," she said a few days later at the White House. "My remarks meant, 'Great, great rally.' They would have been the same had it been the other side. This is what is great about America—it was a very good rally. I would have said the same had it been the prolife people. I was a little disappointed in the reporting of it. I think the slant was not quite fair. I thought it was peaceful, nobody was hurt. What other country can do that?"

Less fuzzy were the Bushes' views on gun control. George, the sportsman hunter, opposed it; Barbara, the childhood mender of broken wings, supported it. Then came the shooting deaths of those five children in a California schoolyard, and Barbara's horrified reaction. She acknowledged that "all of America" had been aware of her off-the-cuff remark that assault rifles should have been outlawed, but she refused to take any credit for George's subsequent turnaround on the issue, culminating in his May 1989 recommendation that their sale be banned.

"I think, you know, one great thing about George is—and I think it's very important—that he's open-minded," she said. "And I think the shooting of those children just was devastating to him. . . . I think he waited and weighed all the facts. And the facts are pretty strong. But I had nothing to do with it."

The discussion led into something else about her that puzzled reporters. Had she decided to "muzzle" herself because she was First Lady?

"No, no, I muzzled myself about 1967 when George went into the Congress," she said. "It's a decision I made many years ago that when I disagreed with George Bush, I tell him in private. Occasionally, I've had slippage, but very rarely."

10

The Feeling's Mutual

"I don't fool around with his office and he doesn't fool around with my household."

mericans probably always suspected that their First Ladies indulged in a little pillow talk, but it took Betty Ford to say as much when she announced that she and her husband would sleep in their own old double bed at the White House. Then along came Rosalynn Carter, who not only shared Jimmy's pillow but his Roosevelt Room cabinet table.

But Rosalynn wasn't the first president's wife to enter that inner sanctum. Barbara Bush remembered the productions Richard Nixon staged for Pat Nixon and the wives of his cabinet. Barbara attended several because George Bush held cabinet rank as the U.S. ambassador to the United Nations. "They did not talk baby talk, but they did not go into a deep cabinet meeting," she told me of the discussions. "It was show biz. I don't think we conquered the world. And nobody asked us to speak, either."

Influence. That coveted yet dreaded word by which Washington power brokers live and against which president's wives are judged. In the twenty-five years the Bushes had been climbing the pyramid of national politics, the influence exerted by First Ladies had come under increasing examination. Lady Bird Johnson's had been unappreciated, Pat Nixon's unperceived, Betty Ford's liberating, and Rosalynn Carter's powerful.

But it was Nancy Reagan's meddlesomeness that Barbara Bush was up against. If there was one question Barbara could expect the media to ask her in the long months of George's campaign, it was the one about influence. Would she influence policy?

"No, I don't think so," she said, then teasingly added, "Who knows?" She said she wasn't so sure that previous First Ladies who had appeared guilty were guilty and seemed to be saying that those who appeared innocent might not have been innocent. "So even a nice innocent like me might," she said, laughing.

Barbara was no game player who engaged in end-run maneuvering; she was direct about her influence and how she used it. Asked about Nancy Reagan's use of Reagan friends and aides to bring pressure on Ronald Reagan, Barbara replied curtly in the January 1989 session with a group of reporters, "We do things differently. I have always been able to go through George."

Former Bush aides like Bush's coauthor Vic Gold, who had dealt with her through the years, attested to that. "You're not going to find Barbara asserting the kind of influence that Nancy Reagan asserted. And you're not going to find Barbara talking to George's friends and saying, 'Can you do something to help' on a situation. If she has anything on her mind, she just expresses it to him. He'll listen and say, 'Well, I'll think about that.' At the same time he is liable to say, 'I just don't see it that way.' "

Her children, with predictable bias, knew her to be strong, even tough, but never a manipulator. "She avoids politics and political issues and sticks with what she's concerned about. I think Americans want a First Lady who won't be active in policy-making but will use her leverage and clout to enhance the lives of others. She is being perceived that way," said Neil Bush soon after his parents moved to the White House, "and the perception of my mother is the reality."

Where George's office was concerned, "I'm a very normal human being," Barbara told me. "If I thought something was hurting George, I would certainly say to him, 'George, I think Jane Smith is doing you a disservice.' I wouldn't say, 'Fire her or fire him.' That's not really the way we work. We have a good marriage. One reason it's good, maybe, is I don't fool around with his office and he doesn't fool around with my household."

Stories about Nancy Reagan's influence at the White House had been a sizzling topic in the spring of 1988. Former White House chief of staff Donald Regan, in his book *For the Record: From Wall Street to Washington,* had outraged Washington with his revelation that Nancy regularly consulted an astrologer about President Reagan's schedule. Barbara Bush told me later she never read horoscopes or went to see astrologers though some of her best friends did. She laughed about one thing someone told her: "I'm Gemini, so's George. We were told we probably should never get married, that Gemini don't get along. So I'll think about it—after forty-three years."

She had a point. There wasn't much the Bushes didn't know about each other. Barbara knew George liked "friends, family, sports" but hated "many green vegetables, people who are negative, anyone who runs down someone he loves. Gossip. Unfairness." She once said they thought alike in many cases, which probably meant that George knew Barbara felt pretty much the same way except perhaps for the green vegetables. They were traditional people with an unorthodox view of situations in which they often found themselves. "Sometimes—well, almost all the time —there'll be an after-dinner speaker who reminds us of something funny," Barbara told the *Christian Science Monitor* in 1984. "I look across at George and get laughing 'cause he knows what I'm thinking and I know exactly how it's going to grab him."

George and Barbara shared everything, communicating by simply looking at one another many times, according to their son Jeb. Barbara gave George much of the credit. "I'm not terribly sympathetic with the theory that political wives have a hard time," she once said. "I think it really depends on the husband. If he shares like George Bush, then everything is possible."

In public, at least, they were easygoing with one another, whether just kidding around or facing ticklish political situations. Barbara more than once just rolled her eyes at one of George's antics. A case in point was a dinner *Time* magazine reported that the Chinese ambassador gave for the Bushes a month before George became president. A lover of gags, George took along a fishing line to which he attached a dollar bill, then dropped it on the floor for an unsuspecting person to pick up. When a waiter tried, George jerked the dollar away and with the ambassador, burst into gales of laughter. Barbara rolled her eyes on that one and according to *Time* magazine, told her host, "You're going to have your work cut out for you with the new administration."

The extent of Barbara's influence on the Bush campaign was always a matter of conjecture to the media and to his aides who scripted it. After George chose Dan Quayle as his running mate, Barbara defended his decision with characteristic fervor, maintaining that George had kept her, like everyone else, in the dark right up to the convention. The Quayles certainly were no strangers to her and she valued the opinions some of her closest friends—like Bush campaign director Jim Baker's wife, Susan, and former

RNC chairman Dean Burch's wife, Pat—had of Marilyn. "They love her and think she is one of the great women, a great family person, a bright lawyer, a good tennis player, a devout practicing Christian—not that that makes a difference, but the devout part I like. She's in a prayer group with a lot of those people. And I like her," Barbara told me during an October 1988 campaign trip. "All that stuff that came out about him [Quayle] was nothing. I think he's better qualified to be Vice President than Mike Dukakis is to be President. I really feel that way. You never know until someone steps up to the bat how they're going to hit, and I think you're going to find he is exceptional."

After the election, what doubts anybody had about Barbara's influence on George's administration soon dissolved. There was evidence of Barbara's touch in three appointments—Dr. Louis H. Sullivan as secretary of Health and Human Services, Jack F. Kemp as secretary of Housing and Urban Development, and William J. Bennett as the administration's new drug czar. All would be leading figures dealing with social problems of particular concern to her.

Since 1982 she had been on the board of trustees of Atlanta's Morehouse College School of Medicine headed by Sullivan, and she had played a major role in its $15-million fund drive. She tapped Sullivan for national attention when she asked him to introduce her at the GOP convention in New Orleans. Sullivan's first lesson in power politics came shortly after

President-elect Bush announced that he intended to nominate him. In an interview with the *Atlanta Journal and Constitution*, the doctor said his position on abortion was freedom of choice. A few days later he restated that position as opposing abortion except in cases of rape, incest, and threat to the woman's life. The switch may have raised questions about his credibility and given antiabortion forces a wedge in winning guarantees of key HHS positions, but he subsequently won Senate confirmation.

As for Bennett and Kemp, Barbara was friendly to both. She was an admitted admirer of Bennett when he was Reagan's education secretary. And despite the fact that Bush and Kemp had opposed each other during the presidential primaries, she liked the former New York congressman. "I think she was a good bridge in helping George Bush see the human side of the Kemps as a family. I think that kind of warmed the relationship to the point where George Bush really wanted to find a place for Jack Kemp," said Craig Fuller.

Bush's campaign advisers already knew never to doubt Barbara's positive influence, both on the approach he took to social issues and on his campaign stump style. "There were telltale signs. The emotional issues, like the homeless and hunger, were all higher on his agenda because of her influence," remembered Sheila Tate, Bush's campaign press secretary. "She questioned the need for tough personal attacks, or those construed as personal, because she didn't like any attack. When she was with him, without fail he would tend to become a kinder, gentler candidate."

But she was no softie in campaign strategy. The afternoon of the Iowa caucuses when George and Barbara knew he was not going to win them, they piled onto Air Force Two and headed for New Hampshire. "Everybody was pretty down and Rich Bond and Lee Atwater were taking full blame. The Vice President said, 'Look, we're going to press on.' And at that point Mrs. Bush said, 'Enough of this. You know, it's over. Everybody go take out a dirty book and start reading,' " Fuller recalled.

She tasted revenge in New Hampshire. Atwater and others had felt airing the so-called "straddle" ad showing Iowa caucus winner Robert J. Dole on two sides of the tax issue was critical to George's strategy in New Hampshire. George was not convinced, despite then-governor John Sununu's opinion that he saw nothing wrong with it. "You may not win if we don't use this ad," Atwater argued. Only when Barbara, who deplored negative advertising, assured George that she thought the ad was all right, did he relent. They ran the ad and George won New Hampshire by ten percentage points.

Though Barbara liked to play down her involvement, Bush aides saw her as a key campaign adviser. She would dismiss the importance of her presence at periodic briefing sessions at Kennebunkport. "George asked me to come in because I'm going to have to feed them and house them," she told me about one such occasion. "I said to Craig, 'I promise you they'll have clean sheets, clean windows to look out of. I will feed them. I hope I can sit in on the meetings.' He said, 'Well, we can't change now'—he was kidding me."

Atwater remembered that she was more than chief cook and bottle washer. He recalled a long weekend in May 1985, the first of Bush's presidential campaign strategy meetings when he and his wife, Sally, were staying in one of the small houses on the Bush compound at Walker's Point. Atwater went jogging, returned sweaty, and wanted a shower. But when he turned it on, he found the water was cold. "I went to the house and there was Barbara. I told her there was no hot water—I figured she'd go tell one of the people. But she grabbed a toolbox, put on one of the Vice President's jackets, and came to the little house. I still thought she was going to call somebody, but she just climbed up on a chair, got her wrench, and started turning until she got the hot water. I felt very feminine just standing there."

Fuller recalled that she was involved from the very beginning in discussions on political strategy— "what we were thinking about in the way of themes and issues. She would sit in on sessions both at Kennebunkport and at the residence, ask questions, offer her advice and counsel, never missing a thing but seldom challenging staff members. Her position was to let George Bush be himself, don't try to overmanage, overcontrol him, let him take questions as often as possible, don't overprogram him."

She was a critical audience of one, not just an adoring spouse listening to her husband on the stump, and she kept track of what he said. If she didn't think his answers were as good as they might have been—about the homeless or the hungry, for instance—she let him know. "They were very constructive suggestions, normally made in private. She would never have walked into a room with ten people and critiqued something," said Fuller, who got a glimpse of how he thought Barbara voiced her opinion in private to George when the three of them were in a limousine driving away from one of the debates. "She said, 'I thought one of the weaker moments was when you were talking about homelessness.' She was equally watchful of literacy and the issue of education. He was saying he wanted to be the education president and she said, 'You ought to be able to elaborate more.' I thought that was probably what happened a great deal between them."

By her own description, early morning in the Bush household, whether at their Washington residence, in Kennebunkport or a hotel room, was often a work session in which she and George discussed issues. "We wake up every morning and read three papers and read aloud things—I more than he, of course, because men don't read aloud the way women do. But he will say here's an article you ought to read, you'll find this interesting. Here's an article about your friend, or about this issue, or here's something you asked me about. Sometimes vice versa," she said.

Though firm about her opinions, she knew the political hazards a candidate's wife faced in talking about issues on the stump. That did not keep her from being a keen observer of what others—including candidates' wives—were saying. And she often said what she thought about such problems as AIDS, affordable housing, catastrophic health and comprehensive health coverage for the aging in "press availabilities" that followed her campaign appearances. She accumulated experts the same way she accumulated friends and didn't hesitate recommending them to George if she thought he could learn something from them. She could say to George, "I visited with this banker and we spent a half-hour talking about affordable housing. I really would like to recommend that you get someone to come down from his group, tell us how it's going, what's happening, and are they financing this."

Something else she and George often talked about was education. She joked that she liked to think that she had contributed something to his attitudes, but she often said, "I'd like to take credit for all those wonderful things, but I can't." She was interested in what she called "spotting children at risk," while George was interested in "the quality of actual curricula." George said you couldn't judge a president's commitment to solving social problems like illiteracy, drugs, and homelessness by the amount of money the federal government spent on them. In tight fiscal times, he believed a president had to "bring out the best" in both the public and private sectors by enlisting their resources. Barbara saw "networking" as one way to go about that.

"That's what's happening in literacy. I'm seeing this in Project Literacy U.S. [PLUS]. The community comes together and says, 'We've got Laubach Literacy Action, Literacy Volunteers of America, the Methodist Church over here doing something in English as a second language.' All of a sudden what you're seeing now is all the literacy programs getting together and working through unemployment and driver's license agencies and libraries and suddenly they're doing a much better job. The government is doing a lot of networking, so when someone is talking about job training, they're also talking about education. They're not competing, but working together."

Barbara saw homelessness as an emerging national issue long before George did, partly because of the work with the homeless and hungry by her good friend Susan Baker, wife of Jim Baker, the old Bush hand who was then White House chief of staff for Ronald Reagan. Among her other efforts, Susan persuaded the Department of Defense to release surplus commissary food to food banks across the country, helped found emergency shelter for the homeless in Washington, and set up a permanent committee known as the Committee for Food and Shelter, Inc. She got other high-level government wives interested, and Barbara credits Susan with bringing the issue to her attention at a cabinet wives meeting. After that, during stops in other cities, Barbara paid secret visits to homeless shelters.

George talked about the homeless in an interview with David Hoffman of the *Washington Post* in April 1988. He told how after one of the debates with other GOP candidates, "some guy that's all involved in one of these homeless programs wrote Barbara saying, 'I know you care about the homeless, but I listen to your husband [and] he doesn't.' So we [Barbara and George] got into a big argument. She had been telling me I had to do more, and I think she's right. I think I have to convey what I feel about it, particularly the kids, the family. But I don't have to then go the next step, which is to stand up and adopt the liberal Democratic agenda of breaking the federal government to do it."

Constructive suggestions were one thing. But Barbara reacted angrily when she thought George was unfairly criticized. A *Newsweek* cover story titled "George Bush: Fighting the 'Wimp Factor' " in October 1987 infuriated her. "It was a cheap shot," she told Claudia Luther of the *Los Angeles Times*. "It hurt. It hurt our children, truthfully. It hurt George's mother. It hurt me. I mean it was hurtful."

Barbara had no trouble at all seeing George's charisma, and she would agree with her husband's own description of himself once to a reporter that "I'm a charismatic son of a gun!"—no matter how Gary Trudeau portrayed him in *Doonesbury*, his nationally syndicated cartoon strip. "People who saw a man who fought for his country, who built a business and added to the productivity of this country, who never turned down his president when he was asked to serve, nobody thought that," she said. "Only one little cartoonist."

As the campaign progressed and the media raised the "wimp factor" to her directly, she flung it right back at her questioners with an impassioned response that the matter was interesting "only to you, baby. Only to you" and a vow that "I'm not going to answer that question anymore, as of this moment. I never want to hear that word again. Any other questions?" George knew all about her combative nature. "She'll go to bat for me, sometimes more than I'm inclined to myself," he had told NBC News in 1984. "She'll take 'em on head-to-head, dog eat dog. And that's fine. I'm glad to have her defending me. I'd rather have her on my side than not. She's been there for forty years."

Barbara sounded like a politician at times in her distrust of the press. She acknowledged that it is "probably necessary," but in the greater scheme of things felt strongly that it "had a really big responsibility to report accurately and fairly" and didn't believe it always met that responsibility. "Occasionally, you wake up and there's terrible press. You think, why should such a wonderful man, why should he take all that?" she told Dave Montgomery of the *Fort Worth Star-Telegram* in early 1987 as questions about Bush's role in the Iran–contra scandal continued to go unanswered. She was equally concerned about the effect Bush's bad press had on her children. "Marvin had his colon taken out last year because he worried about a lot of things," she said. "A lot of them were related to criticism about his father." Marvin Bush, who underwent surgery in 1986 for ulcerative colitis, said later that he did worry about his father and was sensitive to criticism about both his parents, but he ventured that his colitis had nothing to do with politics. "Mom will never be a doctor—I know more about colitis than she does," he said. "I talked to an eleven-year-old who has it, but her dad didn't run for president."

The only time Barbara asked for time off from bad news during the campaign was after George's defeat in the Iowa caucuses. "I didn't ask George not to look at television. I just asked him not to do it in the bedroom," she told me. "It's just hard to go out and campaign for twelve hours when you're hearing such depressing things." She told the *Cincinnati Enquirer* that "in order to be able to survive what a campaign does to you, you have to sometimes stick your head in the sand, like an ostrich, and block it out. George doesn't like me to say it, because it makes you sound like a nincompoop when you say you don't follow the news. But the bad news gets to you, anyway." She described how, after campaigning all day, she sought solitude that week reading paperback novels or watching movies in her hotel room, avoiding the nightly news. "Then I read in the paper that Mrs. Bush reads a book a day—for seven days I read a cheap little novel a day, only seven days—but now I've gone down in history as the world's biggest nut, who never reads the newspapers, never listens to television, and reads a book a day."

There was another hurt she had to endure throughout the campaign, the rumor about George's infidelity. "We were always concerned about how she was going to respond, how to address it. How do you discuss this issue," said Craig Fuller, Bush's chief of staff at the time. "I remember when the question was being asked. We were being killed by rumor and nobody had asked the question of George Bush yet."

A week or two before the *Newsweek* piece came out in which George W. Bush said he had asked his father and was told the rumors weren't true, a trio of Bush's aides called the Vice President to ask if they could have a talk. Fuller and Atwater, then campaign manager, and Robert Teeter, then pollster and strategist, would have preferred being almost anywhere else on earth to sitting there on the front porch at the Vice President's House with George Bush that day.

Fuller remembered that Bush was furious that whole thing was coming up. Up until then, aides followed the strategy of making no comment on a rumor on the theory that as long as nobody talked about it, the media couldn't write it. Time was running out, however, and some course of action had to be agreed upon. About then, Barbara, who had been out walking, came around the corner of the house. Not knowing some kind of damage control action was being planned, she asked what everybody was talking about. Her visitors wanted to dive for cover. So George told her why they had come and what was worrying them. "That's ridiculous, the answer's no.

Forget about it," she scolded. "What are you even talking about it for? Why are you guys even here?"

Her reaction was to the point, practical, and also characteristic of her. She was remarkably good at building confidence, bolstering George and telling people around him to buck up. Said Fuller, "You don't have to be delicate or dance around the point with her. That was just another affirmation, of course, and we then had a kind of sense that they were fine and they were going to take the thing head-on."

They met it in part by using humor. After the Democratic National Convention in Atlanta, some Bush advisers worried that Kitty and Michael Dukakis were scoring points with their public display of affection. Couldn't George pay more attention to Barbara in public? Couldn't they hold hands once in a while? Unaccustomed to wearing their affection, the Bushes came up with a routine that they rehearsed in Kennebunkport and played with perfection a few days later at the GOP convention in New Orleans. Sometimes it ended when Barbara put her head on George's shoulder, sometimes when the two of them walked away from the cameras giving each other a kick in the fanny. When I asked about their lack of public demonstrativeness, Barbara said, "George is very, very affectionate in private, but we are just not—"

"Wait a minute," George interrupted, starting to slide his left arm around her. "You saw me put my arm around you."

"You know, we've been married so long we don't have to do that," she continued, trying to ignore him. "It's fake."

"Sweetie," he cooed, "let's go down life's highway together into the sunset."

"This is the way we sit and read books every night," she said, giving up.

At the convention, George introduced Barbara to several thousand admiring Republican women at a luncheon tribute to her by calling her "sweetie" and giving her a great big smack. She took her cue. "Thank you very, very much"—she paused, then drew out the word—"sweetie," and urged the crowd to "see if he looks at me adoringly as I look at him" as George took a seat on the dais behind her.

In serious moments, they admitted they weren't publicly sentimental. Barbara defended her comment that hand-holding was "phony," a remark that could as easily have been aimed at Nancy and Ronald Reagan as at Kitty and Michael Dukakis. "They asked me why George Bush didn't show more affection to me. I said that would be phony, all that hand-holding. He and I are very affectionate in our own way. We are the most happily married couple. We don't have to pretend for people."

Said Nancy Ellis, George's sister, "The Kennedys weren't demonstrative. I think it's kind of sticky to be sentimental, you know, sort of tasteless, don't you? I mean, I don't think you want to see them kissing—when you've been married for forty-five years a certain amount of comfortableness sets in where you don't go rushing around and kissing every minute."

But George did put his feelings about her on the record.

There was the time he told me, "If Barbara Bush would ever run for office, I'd like to be her campaign manager."

And the 1988 campaign video, which he ended by saying, "If I weren't George Bush, who would I like to be? Barbara Bush's second husband."

And the Barbara Walters interview, when he described her as "a kind and strong and a loving person whose priorities are her family, her garden, her faith, who will be totally unspoiled by being First Lady of the land, and will emerge no matter what we do after this, happy."

"I like the picture," said Barbara Bush, taking it all in.

11

White House Circles

*"You know, politics has been very good
for us as a family."*

*G*eorge Bush, dressed in his white tie and tails, was ready to go when Barbara came out of the bedroom the night of April 1, 1989. "Oh, surely you're not going to wear that," he twitted, noticing the strawberry-blond wig on her head. "You don't have the nerve!"

"Oh, yes, I do," said Barbara, heading for the door. "Let's go!"

Their Secret Service agents and the White House staff did a double take as the Bushes got off the elevator and walked out to the presidential limousine. When they arrived at the Capitol Hilton three blocks away, the welcoming committee included still more

Secret Service agents and the president of the Gridiron Club.

Lawrence M. O'Rourke, a twenty-five-year veteran of covering the White House as correspondent and columnist for the *St. Louis Post Dispatch,* certainly knew President George Bush when he saw him. The woman getting out of the car with him, however, looked like a stranger. People were confused, and O'Rourke, embarrassed, was about ready to ask Bush who she was when suddenly it dawned on him that he had seen that face somewhere before—in fact, at the White House only that day when Bush dedicated the new regulation-size horseshoe pit near the swimming pool. Recovering, O'Rourke said, "Welcome, Mrs. Bush," and led the way to a hotel holding room where Vice President Dan Quayle and his wife, Marilyn, were waiting.

Dan, who would later joke to Barbara that "we missed you at the Gridiron," looked perplexed when he saw her. Not Marilyn, who was only too familiar with Barbara's "wicked wit," having known her since 1981 when as Second Lady she automatically led the Senate Ladies group to which the wife of then Senator Dan Quayle belonged. "Barbara, what have you done to your hair?" Marilyn asked, and that was all that it took for the two of them and Pat O'Rourke to start laughing. They recognized it as a stunning joke Barbara was about to pull off before the club's 60 very important Washington journalists and their 570 equally important guests at the annual Gridiron dinner.

Some people got it—"You're so brave, you're so brave," Swedish ambassador Wilhelm Wachtmeister said over and over as she sat between him and Supreme Court associate justice William J. Brennan, Jr., at the head table. Some people thought they got it and were waiting for her to flip her wig into the audience and emerge as her white-haired self again. Some just never got it and thought the worst—that because of the thyroid problem she had disclosed a few days earlier she was undergoing radiation treatment and had lost her hair.

"Luckily," said George, playing straight man to his wife in his remarks to the crowd, "Barbara has not reacted in the slightest to all the comments about her gray hair."

The last time a First Lady had stolen the show was in 1982. That night Nancy Reagan brought down the same house with her "Second Hand Rose" number poking fun at her own imperial ways and clotheshorse image. Nancy's aim had been a calculated step to soften up that hard-boiled crowd of movers and shakers as part of a systematic public relations effort to humanize her after months of criticism.

Barbara's aim was simply Barbara's having the last laugh—just as she usually had the last word—after years of hearing jokes about her hair. Anybody familiar with the Gridiron's satiric musical revue, in which official Washington is "singed but never burned," could have figured out that at least one song at Barbara's expense was inevitable, and there had also been that night when Cheryl Arvidson of the

Dallas Times came on stage wearing a big blue dress and a white wig to sing a parody of "Pistol Packin' Momma" that went "lay that Uzi down, George, lay that Uzi down." Barbara had been a guest at enough of those dinners to know that VIP egos were put on the spit and left to turn slowly, slowly in the din of laughter.

Afterward, she was happy enough with the effect the wig created—except "the color could have been a little lighter, but then I wasn't going for a beauty contest." She told me she had thought about doing it for a long time, then this year "it just struck me. It was something that amused me . . . I thought I'm just tired of the hair, talking about it. I'll just wear a wig and see how they like me in that."

She was also weary of the attention given her after she disclosed she had Graves' disease, a condition commonly known as hyperthyroidism, and would undergo radiation treatment to destroy her thyroid gland, which was producing excessive levels of hormone. "Now please," she kidded reporters when she made the announcement, "don't have me dying." She'd had a "small argument" with her press secretary about whether the treatment was anybody's business, though she knew she had to be forthcoming. Almost certainly somebody would notice that she had lost weight since the campaign—twenty-one pounds to be exact—and would wonder if she were dieting, had gone to a fat farm, or was ill.

"I feel it would be better if three months from now we had said, 'She's totally over the problem, the radiation worked and all is well,' " she said. But with the story out, there was no way she could avoid the well-meaning but nonetheless bothersome questions about her health, no matter what the occasion, including the time she had Sweden's queen, Silvia, over to tea at the White House. "Instead," complained Barbara, "standing in a receiving line, two hundred people ask me how I feel—only because they love me and they're kind. But it takes an emphasis off Queen Silvia or anything else I'm doing."

What tickled Barbara were the jokes. She thought George's playing to people's fear of radiation especially funny, particularly the one he told a Union, New Jersey, audience that she had gotten "a clean bill of health" from Walter Reed Hospital but that he was taking another look at their doctor. "He told her it's okay to kiss your husband but don't kiss the dog." "Actually," Barbara chuckled, "I'm a big kisser and you can see people turning a cheek instead, afraid I'm going to get 'em!"

The best part of her April Fools' Day gag, it turned out, was the side effect she hadn't expected. "Not one living human asked me how I felt, and it was an enormous relief. I mean, to go around to people and say, 'I'm really sorry, I feel well,' is so boring."

The turnabout was vintage Barbara Bush, having the time of her life at a time in her life when she could do and say just about anything she wanted. The White House had become Barbara's window on the world, with views in all directions.

One especially commanding view was from the White House tennis court where Barbara tried to keep long-standing twice weekly dates with her tennis regulars, among them Supreme Court Associate Justice Sandra Day O'Connor and longtime friend Andy Stewart. She said she liked swimming better, that her tennis was "so bad." One reason may have been the distractions from the court. "You're looking at the Washington Monument on one side and the White House on the other. And the trees are so spectacular."

It was difficult to imagine how anyone who lived in this historic house amid such a magnificent setting could ever be unhappy there. Barbara's sympathies had gone out to Nancy Reagan more than once over the eight years that the White House had been her home and where she sometimes felt besieged. When John Hinckley tried to kill President Reagan in March 1981, barely two months after the Reagans had moved in, Barbara said she "felt sick for our country and so wanted to help Nancy, but I knew she needed her closest friends." If there was a lesson at all from that day, Barbara said it was the realization "that President Reagan was strong. Thank God. We knew—and know—that it is a risky job." There had been moments at the Vice President's House when Barbara said she, too, had felt hemmed in but she could change into her running suit and take the dog for a walk knowing there was no one around. Nancy lived in a far more public place and Barbara said she once remarked about that to her. "I turned around and Nancy had tears in her eyes. She said something about 'two hundred people had passes to our house so you could hardly wear a bathrobe, and you can't walk outside on your lawn.' "

When Barbara Bush reached 1600 Pennsylvania Avenue, she found that people still had passes and that she couldn't wear her bathrobe in some parts of the White House. But she could take walks on the lawn outside, and she made a daily habit of circling the driveway at least once. It was not Barbara's nature to feel besieged; she was overjoyed by her surroundings and like George wanted to share them with as many people as possible. He once pulled a Newcastle, Massachusetts, woman and four children out of the White House tour line to show them Millie's puppies "as a little dividend for waiting in line," he said, prompting Gary Trudeau in *Doonesbury* to note wryly, "Not even visitors on the White House tour are considered safe."

Certainly few presidents in modern times had been as persistent with their hospitality. In as many days, the Bushes hosted nearly one hundred events as varied as black-tie dinners, Friday nights at the movies, and hot dogs and horseshoes on the South Lawn. In fact, the flow of people into the mansion was so steady that during lunch one day when George and Barbara were talking about still others they wanted to have over, she called the chief usher up to ask if they were working the staff too hard. Telling a friend about it later, she said he replied, "Well, Mrs. Bush, you've had forty-eight occasions since the start of the term. We can handle that for a while. But if we're still going at that pace in October, we won't have anybody working for us." She couldn't help noticing that throughout the entire discussion, George went right on writing down names on his yellow pad.

"Pearl Mesta Bush," as Barbara nicknamed her husband, drew up their guest lists from politics, business, academia, sports, the arts, government, and the clergy. There were authors, cartoonists, governors, judges, board chairmen, publishers, cabinet officers, actors, singers, clergymen and coaches, and just about anybody else who came to George Bush's mind. There was also George's core group of early Republican supporters in the House and Senate.

Everyone who knew the Bushes expected nothing less. They had always turned to their circles from Rye and Greenwich, from Yale and Kennebunkport, Odessa and Midland, Houston, Washington, New York, and Beijing to satisfy a need to relax with people they liked and trusted. "Neither George nor I could live without friends," said Barbara. Now at the White House, drawing from those concentric circles that were widening day by day, they tapped friends who could help them stay informed, keep current, stave off isolation, and most importantly, in whom they could bank a little political capital that George might be able to count on as the going got tough.

"Other politicians may draw a line between real friends and political friends; the Bushes do not," observed Maureen Dowd in the *New York Times*. Doro LeBlond, who as a child knew no other way of life than being surrounded by her parents' expanded family, said living in the White House probably could be isolating. "But over my parents' dead bodies!"

George's affable nature and Barbara's folksy hospitality that could put anybody at ease had made them the quintessential couple long before their return address was The White House. They exuded warmth and conviviality. "Dad and Mom make it fun. They have great senses of humor. Everything is relaxed. There is always some activity going on," Doro said.

For those sometimes dazzled objects of the Bushes' affections, the intimacy of inclusion was an experience even the most jaded could not resist. "This sounds kind of crass, but George Bush is more of a buddy, as opposed to being a president," Representative Gerald B.H. Solomon of New York, a Republican, told Dowd. "We looked at Ronald Reagan with so much awe, but George Bush just seems more like one of you."

Democrats, too, had to hand it to Bush. "This is a company town. George Bush shops at the company store. He knows what's sold there," said Robert S. Strauss, as former chairman of the Democratic National Committee, Mr. Democrat himself. Reported Ellen Warren of Knight-Ridder: "Even retired House Speaker Tip O'Neill, the consummate Democrat, confided recently to an acquaintance, 'I love the Bushes.' "

The press, too, which had been pointedly excluded from most of the Bushes' 1,192 breakfasts, luncheons, receptions, and dinners at the vice presi-

dent's mansion, began to receive written or tele-
phoned invitations to the White House. Barbara
Feinman, writing for the *Washington Post* in November 1988, reported that though the Bushes received a
congressional allocation of $258,000 annually to
maintain the residence and to entertain, they turned
down her request to explain how the money was spent
because while George was Vice President Barbara
Bush regarded the parties they gave as "private."

The care the Bushes took never to publicly up-
stage the Reagans contributed to their no-press policy.
By staying out of the limelight they had avoided tire-
some, if not embarrassing, comparisons—their at-
home way of entertaining with the glamorous style
of the Reagans, by definition Washington's—and the
nation's—preeminent host and hostess.

Such caution was no longer necessary—or always possible—after the Bushes made the two-mile
move to the White House. There was media coverage
of state and official dinners in the State Dining
Room—the first three that spring were for the leaders
of Egypt, Israel, and Jordan—highly formal affairs
that Barbara Bush once told me she looked upon more
as "photo opportunities" for the benefit of the American public than as occasions where business was
transacted.

But the vast majority of the Bushes' parties, upstairs in the family quarters, went unreported by the
media, even though some of its representatives were
there. For journalists invited as guests, it was understood that the parties were off-the-record, which

meant that what everybody talked about was not for publication. Five nights after the Bushes moved in, they gave their first dinner in their upstairs family dining room—for United Nations Secretary General Javier Perez de Cuellar and his wife, Marcela, a symbolic gesture to the international community but also a friendly one stemming back to Bush's days at the United Nations. Kathy Lewis of the *Houston Post* was one of three journalists invited that night who knew to leave her notebook at home. Though such invitations would later touch off a mild debate about whether working press should ever be nonworking guests of a president, Lewis said she never considered declining. "I feel I am responsible for my own integrity and credibility, and I considered it an opportunity—a fairly rare one—to spend an evening with a number of news sources." She saw it as a situation not dissimilar to being a guest at an official White House dinner, as many of her media colleagues had been under previous presidents, although those dinners were not off-the-record since working press were allowed to cover them.

What surprised Lewis about the Bushes' dinner was that she wasn't the only one among the thirty-eight guests—several famous and others simply politically important to any administration—who had never been upstairs where the President lived or seen the historic Queen's and Lincoln bedrooms there. That dinner, emphasizing hospitality as much as protocol, set the tone for the dozens the Bushes gave in succeeding weeks.

An evening *en famille* with the Bushes invariably began with a personally conducted tour of the family quarters, complete with damp bathroom towels and Barbara's face powder. George provided the commentary, with needling asides by Barbara. Sometimes the guests sat on the Lincoln bed while the President aimed the Polaroid. Asked at one point if they were ever alone at the dinner table, Barbara herself had trouble remembering. If they were, as Lewis later wrote, the occasion went largely unnoticed.

The same was true of lunchtime. Barbara gave nonstop luncheons in the family dining room, some for friends, others to publicize causes she believed in. No one left without a personally conducted tour or having his picture taken. In May 1989, she entertained several of her old friends from the 90th Congress group who still got together regularly. Shirley Pettis Roberson, her old Palisade Lane neighbor, flew in from California and like many of the Bushes' friends coming from out of town, was invited to stay at the White House, an unmistakable sign of favored-friend status.

"We all had to pinch ourselves that one of us, who started in Washington twenty-three years ago, was now in the White House," said Antoinette Hatfield, whose husband, Mark, had entered the U.S. Senate from Oregon the same year that George Bush entered the U.S. House of Representatives from Texas. "She was no different than she had been when she was showing us her first house from top to bottom. She's still as orderly, organized, and disciplined as ever. She was always the one who played tennis regularly, who did needlepoint and finished what she started while the rest of us had two or three projects going, the one who always wrote thank-yous in response to anything you did or sent to her."

What also came across to these women was that Barbara Bush might be First Lady, but she seemed unchanged as their friend, as loyal to them in 1989 as she had been twenty years earlier when she was visiting the White House for the first time as a congressional wife, never dreaming she would be living there herself someday. "We realized she has good friends like all of us in all parts of this country, in all segments of society, and that she doesn't treat them any differently than she treats us because she cares about people, about what's happening to them and what's happening to their families," said Antoinette Hatfield. "When you're surrounded by a strong and loving family the way Barbara is, you can also give a lot of love."

That family again. As David Maraniss wrote in the *Washington Post* in January 1989, the Bushes, unlike the contemporary American family in which "the patterns of familial discord are so common as to become clichéd . . . are a happy family in a distinct way. Each child has had something to overcome—George his father's name, Jeb his early disaffectedness, Neil his reading disability, Marvin a life-threatening illness, and Doro her innate shyness. Interestingly, each has overcome by drawing on the traits of the parents."

After the inauguration in 1989, the five Bush

children and their children, as well as in-laws and cousins, were as welcome as ever at home. There had been a lot of laughs on that high road to high office, but few ever knew about the tears. "I'd get really upset and call her," said Doro LeBlond, remembering back to the stories about George and the wimp factor, and George and his marital fidelity. "I'd call her and say, 'Well, Mom, did you read that?' And she'd say, 'Yeah, it's awful, but now remember, Doro, this comes with the job.' "

Said Barbara Bush of Doro in May 1988, "She used to be shy but now we're all saying, 'Doro, you've gotten positively aggressive.' She's gotten to be a big politician now, but that doesn't mean she hasn't gotten a tear or two. You know, politics has been very good for us as a family."

At the invitation of son George W., who had bought the Texas Rangers baseball club only a few weeks earlier, Barbara Bush flew to Texas in May 1989 to throw out the first ball of the Rangers' season. George W. was struck by how quickly she figured out the picture he hoped would make the news. "In her Ranger jacket, doing her thing, she knew exactly what to do, and we did a couple of poses together that worked.

"My mother is very good at getting and sending a message to average Americans, and that is because she is just herself," he said. "She is funny, she is glib. There's nothing phony about Barbara Bush. Stylistically, Mother feels more natural in front of cameras, which is not to say that George Bush doesn't. I've just noticed from my impressions that there's a little more showmanship in Mother, and that she's good at it."

The woman who never thought she could speak to the garden club was now seen by her oldest son as "a genius with the media," as "better with the press than Dad is." She'd been learning how all her married life, honing a natural talent, in particular after she returned from China in 1975 and went on the lecture circuit to raise money for her humanitarian causes.

And to marshal support for George.

Nancy Ellis, with the perspective of family memory, was frank in talking about Barbara's part in George's fortunes and misfortunes. She said that George was always well aware that she was a tremendous help to his life; he had written his mother about that, about what Barbara had done for him and meant to him. And Barbara had been generous with her own good fortune—"good about sharing him with all the family, always welcoming us in." That unity had made endurable the tough lessons of Washington life—"I'm still learning," said Barbara in 1989—that snared many a public figure as he worked his way up in Washington and on more than one occasion dragged him down.

"Oh, it was a lucky day for George when he found her," Nancy Ellis said. "She's indomitable. Maybe he'd never be where he is today without her."

Now it was George Bush and his family's turn to share Barbara Bush, a woman who her children believed came into the nation's conscience at just the right time. Neil called her "healthy medicine for America"; George W. said she was "totally honest"; Jeb said she was like "significant numbers of other women her age coming into their own"; Doro said she could be "running Macy's." Marvin saw something of Eleanor Roosevelt in her—"I don't know a whole lot about Eleanor Roosevelt, but I know she was someone who cared about other people a great deal. My mom shares that with her—though I think she's better looking than Eleanor."

In that group interview we had with Barbara a few days before George Bush was sworn in as president, it seemed only fitting to point out to his wife how far she had come. "You're going down in history now," I noted.

There was the suggestion of a shrug and a glimmer of a smile.

"That's not bad, is it?" Barbara Bush agreed.

Index